Praise for

HIDDEN HELL
Discovering My Father's POW Diary

"Robert Miller writes in this memorable and moving book that his father 'went to hell and back and then lived to tell no one but my mom about it.' What he is referring to are his father's experiences as a POW during World War II. Fortunately for us all, we now have a chronicle of what happened to him, how he survived, and his extraordinary vow to forgive."

—SUSAN EISENHOWER, author of *Mrs. Ike*

"A heartfelt and compelling must-read, *Hidden Hell* delves deeply into the horrors of war and the power of PTSD to haunt a soldier for the rest of his life. Readers will be casting the movie before they reach the end of this poignant and beautifully written story."

—BOB WOODRUFF, ABC News (New York)

"'Disrupt the enemies' activities by escaping, when taken prisoner,' is a standard order by the U.S. Armed Services. But how many of us had the guts to ingeniously follow that order? Here is an amazing and powerful story, told in riveting chapters, of a U.S. Private First Class who did it twice and endured the brutal punishment. Readers will be thrilled, shaken, and uplifted. I was."

—DR. GUY STERN
Distinguished Professor Emeritus, Wayne State University and Master Sergeant, WWII (one of the Ritchie Boys)

"What makes this particular war memoir so compelling is that it is driven by a son's need to understand his father. Through his quest, Robert Miller ultimately reaches a better understanding of humanity as a whole and of our conflicted capacity to treat each other with both unspeakable cruelty and redeeming, life-saving compassion."

—JOE FAB, Emmy-nominated producer, writer, and director

Eleanore Kurowski and Herbert Miller shortly before their wedding in 1945.

HIDDEN HELL

Discovering My Father's POW Diary

Robert H. Miller

PUBLISHING
Post Office Box 482
New Hope, PA 18938
Phone: (772) 546-9891
PattonPublishing.com

Printed in the United States of America

Cover and book design: Nancy Rabitoy of Better Direction Design
Editor: Penny Schreiber

Library of Congress Control Number: 2011923890
ISBN: 978-0-9846374-0-9

www.roberthmiller.com

FOR MY FATHER AND MOTHER
AND FOR HEINZ

CONTENTS

FOREWORD

The war of American infantryman Herbert H. Miller lasted little more than a year. But he was a keen witness to the events presented in this fascinating book. Written by his son, Robert, it vividly depicts the real-life experiences of a soldier whose life was turned upside down by the vicissitudes of war and all its unimaginable horrors.

Landing on Omaha Beach on June 11, 1944, Miller immediately confronted the precariousness of life as he participated in the dramatic events that came to be known as the Battle for Normandy. It was the advance of the 30th Infantry Division that placed him at the front lines of Operation Cobra and amid the first hours of the massive counterattack on Hitler's troops at Mortain, France.

On August 6, the first day of the Battle of Mortain, Miller was taken prisoner by the Nazis. He began a cruel two-month march to a German prisoner-of-war camp. After arriving at Stalag VIIA, Miller endured eight more horrifying months as a POW, during which he escaped twice and was twice tortured. Herbert Miller was not a hot-headed or impulsive man but merely a person who suddenly found himself in a deadly situation. He was terrified but determined to survive and complete the task that had been handed to him, a simple soldier.

In May 1945, Miller was liberated by the Allies and the Red Cross, and the following month he returned home to his family. He married his sweetheart, Eleanore, on August 25, 1945. But the war was never really over for Herb Miller. He spoke of his war experiences only to Eleanore, but he suffered from post-traumatic stress disorder for the rest of his life. The week before his death, in 1994, Miller had his last nightmare about the war.

It was only after Herbert's death that his son, Robert, discovered his Red Cross POW diary. It became the catalyst for him to learn about and understand more fully his father's painful wartime experiences and how they had affected his behavior. With his mother's help and strong support, Robert set off to do research and pursue witness accounts during frequent trips to Europe. Slowly and painstakingly he was able to reconstruct the dramatic story of his father's war.

This tender and searing account is dedicated to the memory of Robert's father. And it is dedicated to his late mother, Eleanore, whose unconditional love for her husband sustained him throughout every difficult moment of his post-war life. Finally, it is dedicated to the kind and principled German guard Heinz, who befriended Herbert and looked out for him at Stalag VIIA.

In spring 2008 I met Robert during one of his visits to Mortain. His extraordinary enthusiasm for recording a lasting memory of his father began a special and enduring friendship between the town of Mortain and this son of one of our American liberators.

Herbert Miller will rest eternally in our memories.

Noel Sarrazin, President
European Association of the 30th Infantry
Mortain, France

THOUGHTS FROM HELEN PATTON

I was seven years old and very excited to be spending the summer of 1969 at Green Meadows Farm. George S. Patton Jr. and his wife, Beatrice, had purchased this gorgeous New England estate north of Boston in 1928. They didn't spend a lot of time there until World War II, when Beatrice took up residence and welcomed her children and grandchildren while the old man was at war in Europe.

The Pattons were my grandparents. Our family visits took place many years after both had died, but the sprawling clapboard house was so little changed it seemed as if they'd be back any minute. Grandpa's whiskey was still in the decanter, and Grandma's pen lay neatly on a monogrammed almost-finished thank-you note.

My grandparents had been great collectors, and treasures for children to discover abounded in their house: a stuffed blowfish; a mummy's toe; Marie Antoinette's beauty marks (they still stuck); pistols; muskets; a sombrero that I imagined had been Pancho Villa's; shiny dented helmets with two, three, or four stars; and boatloads of medals. A cannon and a bronze bust of Hitler adorned the lawn. My grandfather had trained his famous bull terrier, Willy, to pee on Hitler.

On a quiet afternoon that summer of 1969 I decided it was finally time to lift the lid on the big black sea chest George and Beatrice had purchased on their honeymoon in 1910. Draped over the chest was a velvet throw. Its precisely faded creases told me I was the first to dare to peek inside. My mother soon came upon me plopped on the living room floor. I was an island surrounded by a sea of black and white photos, stills my grandfather had taken during the liberation of Buchenwald. Staring at me from every direction were hundreds of pictures of gaunt and mutilated rubbery white corpses.

The question "Why?" kept going through my mind. I now had my marching orders for life. My mission: to make the world a better place and to look for answers to that terrible question. To this day, the only thing more shocking to me than those images is any suggestion they are not shocking.

It wasn't until I read Robert Miller's tribute to his POW father that I truly began to comprehend my grandfather's war. Herbert Miller and George Patton had been in close proximity to one another in August 1944. General Patton's Third Army got its go-word to break from Avranches, France, on August 3, just three days before Herbert Miller was captured by the Germans near St. Lô.

Had my grandfather known what was happening to Herbert, he would have sent his troops faster into France, for nothing meant more to him than the well-being of an individual soldier. If he had understood what was taking place in the German concentration camps, I am certain he would have picked up even more speed. My grandfather would surely have been amazed at the resilience of his fellow humans—the men and women in the German POW and concentration camps who surpassed the limits of their bodies and minds to survive through unspeakable terror and torture. In the words of Shakespeare's Hamlet, "What a piece of work is a man."

George Patton and Herbert Miller both believed they'd returned from the war with something worth saving. Herbert placed the Red Cross diary that contained the memories of his terrible year at the back of a dresser drawer. My grandfather put his photos of the liberation of Buchenwald in an old trunk. They had their reasons for preserving these relics of evil.

Throughout his postwar life, Herbert's memories sat silent in that drawer, but the personal traumas connected to them were never safe and sound within him. Robert Miller's story of his father's agonizing and courageous battle to overcome his experiences as a POW can begin to bring closure for us all.

Robert Miller spends many weeks every year working in Germany and France. He embodies his father's determination to forgive, understanding there is no end to war until healing begins.

Helen Patton
Founder and CEO of the Patton Foundation
and the Patton Stiftung Sustainable Trust

PREFACE

This is the remarkable story of my father, Herbert Henry Miller, who was drafted into the army in August 1942. Dad was twenty-one in February 1944 when he boarded the S.S. Argentina in Boston Harbor with the 30th Infantry Division, bound for the European war. He left behind his parents, his brother, two sisters, and the lovely young woman, Eleanore Kurowski, he had fallen in love with only months before. A photo of Eleanore taped to the inside of his undershirt sustained him throughout the ordeals to come.

Dad landed on Omaha Beach on June 11, five days after the mass assault of D-Day. The 30th moved inland, suffering horrific casualties in three major operations, including the gruesome battles of St. LO and Operation Cobra. Captured by the Germans at Mortain on August 6, Dad endured a punishing fifty-four-day march to Moosburg, Germany, where he survived for seven months in Stalag VIIA, the largest POW camp in Nazi Germany. Originally designed to hold 10,000 prisoners, the camp was bursting at the seams by spring 1945, with over 70,000 human souls. The overcrowded conditions led to an increase in dysentery, a mass outbreak of typhus, and widespread death. Stalag VIIA bore no resemblance to the fun-loving place depicted in the 1970s American TV show Hogan's Heroes.

While a prisoner of Nazi Germany, Dad was starved and forced to participate in work details in the city of Munich. Placed on trains and locked in for the three-hour ride, the men experienced frostbite, unsanitary conditions, and almost constant strafing by friendly fire. Early in his time at Stalag VIIA, the work-detail train took a direct hit from American bombs, and my father narrowly escaped death. Several of his buddies were not so lucky.

During his stay at the prison camp, my father became good friends with a Nazi guard named Heinz. Ironically, Heinz had been the German soldier who'd originally taken him captive in France. One day near the end of the war Heinz disappeared from the camp. My father and his friends never saw him again. They came to believe that Heinz had been murdered by his fellow Nazis. My father's friendship with this kind and decent German man haunted him for the rest of his life.

Twice my father planned an escape from Stalag VIIA with his close friend and fellow West Virginian Bert Cottrell. After their first escape both were recaptured in short order, landing in solitary confinement for five days with no food and just enough water to survive. Their second escape involved five other POWs, and it too was a failure. Recaptured by the Nazis, my father's group included two Russian prisoners who were promptly executed in cold blood. My dad, along with the others, was immediately transferred to another camp south of Salzburg, Austria, called Stalag XVIIIC. Bent on revenge, the Nazis placed their captives back in solitary confinement, this time putting each man in his own hole in the ground lined with sharp-pointed branches. The POWs were forced to stand in place for twenty-four hours while deprived of food and water.

Shaken but not broken, Dad endured six more grueling weeks of captivity. Finally, on May 12, 1945, he and the others were liberated by the Allies and the Red Cross and returned to the U.S. Army, becoming free men once again.

PROLOGUE

In 1994 it was estimated that 1,200 World War II veterans were dying every day in America. My father, Herbert Henry Miller, joined the ranks of the deceased veterans on February 9, 1994, when he died suddenly at age seventy-two.

On the bitter cold morning of February 14, I stood shivering at my father's gravesite. My mother, Eleanore, was close by my side as we awaited the arrival of his casket. Memories of my dad flooded my mind. I replayed our life together, reviewing his unique qualities and marveling at how hard he had tried to make my life perfect when I was a young boy.

I glanced down at my mother, who was shaking from the extreme cold. I could feel the sadness radiating from her body as I pulled her tighter against me. My wife, Colleen, pregnant with our son Patrick, walked over to stand at my mother's other side to shield her from the wind. Our four children, Robbie, Shannon, Annemarie, and Christine, all under age eleven and doing their best to be brave and strong, were fidgeting and bouncing around the gravesite, trying to stay warm. No one spoke. The only sounds were the snow crunching under the children's boots, the cry of a lone crow off in the distance, and the wind whistling past our exposed ears.

Off in the distance, we could see the burial tractor heading toward us with my father's casket tucked inside a large golden burial vault suspended from chains. As the tractor approached the new gravesite, the smoke from its exhaust, combined with the cold air, made it look like an old-fashioned train arriving at a railway station. Looking down, I saw how precisely the hole had been dug in the frozen earth. Dad's grave was a work of art. My mother turned to me, saying, "That's one nice gravesite." If my father had been standing there with us, he wouldn't have noticed its perfection. Dad lived his life mostly unaware that the real beauty of things is in the details. This always amazed me, because I am very different.

The burial vault was carefully lined up next to the grave, and we all bent down to pick up pieces of frozen dirt. We could feel the vibration and hear the thud as Dad's vault struck the ground at the bottom of the grave. Anxious to be first, Annemarie tossed in her ball of dirt. Following her lead, we all recited the Lord's Prayer and threw our dirt into the grave, committing my father's body to eternal rest. We walked back to the limousine in tears and headed for the funeral luncheon to be with our family and guests.

DISCOVERING THE DIARY

A few weeks later, I was helping my mother sort through my dad's belongings. Deep in the back of a drawer, she pulled out a wrapped package. Not remembering exactly what it was, she untied the string and undid the paper that encased a worn, light brown, heavily soiled book. Before she had finished, her face filled with emotion and she gasped, "Oh my word, I had forgotten about his book."

My mother had pulled from the back of the drawer my dad's journal from the nine months he spent as a prisoner of war in World War II. She immediately handed it to me. Totally amazed to be holding something I'd never seen or heard of before, I instantly understood that the journal was the missing link to the mystery of my father's war. It would lead me to an understanding of how complex and horrific his experiences had been. It would also lead me to a better understanding of him. The journal was crammed full of his dreams for survival and of the death and destruction he had witnessed. Along with the text, he had scribbled some drawings to help him capture his true feelings. Glancing through it for the first time, I found the name of the prison camp: Stalag VIIA, Moosburg, Germany.

As I reviewed the journal over the next few weeks, I realized that Dad often wrote in it while he was under duress, always careful to avoid the prying eyes of the Nazi guards. I could tell he was frequently interrupted by bombings or guards coming by as he struggled to get his thoughts out on paper. Dad was careful not to comment in his journal on the harsh treatment he received from the Nazis. At the camp, he kept his journal tucked away under the floorboards so it would not be discovered and used against him. As I searched through the maze of text and drawings, I found the chapter that explained how he had come by the journal.

On September 28, 1944, Dad had already been a prisoner of war for fifty-two days. On that day he and his fellow POWs left the small town of Augsburg, Germany, under heavy Nazi guard and were moving toward the ultimate goal of reaching Stalag VIIA. That evening, as they made camp, the POWs heard German trucks heading in their direction. Two stopped at their camp. Inside one truck were thirty Red Cross boxes loaded with food. The POWs were starving, having barely eaten anything for two months.

Dad tore open his box and dug into the rations. Rummaging deeper, he discovered at the bottom of the box a war log created by the YMCA. It did not take long for the others to find theirs as well. The Red Cross was distributing these logs, believing it was good therapy for a soldier to have a diary to help pass the time in captivity. Unfortunately, my father later told my mother, the war logs received mixed reviews from the POWs. Many of them felt permanently embittered by their experiences, saying, "No way—why would I ever want to remember this?"

Dad estimated that many of the unopened journals went into the fire that night. But he decided to keep his. You see, my dad loved to draw and keep busy with his hands, so the journal was perfect for him. In it he would record the story of his long march into Germany as well as the day-to-day details of his time at Stalag VIIA.

On that day when he found the journal in his Red Cross box, he stuffed it down the back of his pants. He later told my mother that it helped to hold them up after all of the weight he'd lost. Dad also told her that he believed none of the senior guards realized that the POWs were finding diaries in their Red Cross boxes, because they were too busy drinking the wine they'd stolen from the French. The POWs' campfire that night burned far longer than usual—all of those discarded war diaries were keeping them warm for once.

Today there are not many POW war diaries in existence. The International Red Cross and the YMCA estimate that one survived for every 500 soldiers captured. Finding my dad's war journal was the catalyst for me to begin my own journey to understand him. As I continued to explore its pages, I was enthralled and captivated by what I was discovering. There were things I could never figure out about him, so many missing pieces to the puzzle of my dad. I was beginning to slowly understand him better now. He had been a fighter, a very stubborn survivor, and even a hero. My dad's experiences during the war, which he never shared with me, indelibly shaped the rest of his life. My father's war journal, in my opinion, is a treasure.

From my earliest childhood, I realized that my dad was different from other people. I also knew that he was keeping a secret. When I was eight, I woke up in the middle of a summer night and overheard my dad's voice. He was in a state of panic and sounded confused. My mom was frantically trying to comfort him, telling him it was a nightmare and he would be OK. "Wake up, wake up!" she kept saying. A short time later, I heard the words "prisoner of war" for the first time. What did they mean? I wondered. Why was my dad so upset? I had never heard my dad cry before, and this night made a deep impression on me. I knew something was very wrong. Afraid and scared, I turned over in my bed and smashed the pillow against my ears, trying to drown out their conversation. Somehow I fell back to sleep.

The next day I thought over what had happened the night before. I knew what a prisoner was, because my friends and I always took the neighborhood girls prisoner when we played war. Had my dad seen prisoners being taken? Did he take prisoners? Is this what was making him sad? I knew he had been in the army, but I had never given any thought to what he had experienced in the war. A sudden realization swept over me. I could hardly believe what my mind was telling me. My dad *was* the prisoner. That was my dad's secret and I needed to find my mom to get more details.

I remember thinking, as I ran to find my mom, just how cool it was going to be to tell my friends about my dad. Nobody else had a dad like mine, and I would have the best story in the neighborhood. I felt strangely proud and confused at the same time. But then I remembered how sad my dad had been in the night. This permanently snuffed out the "cool" factor.

My mom was outside hanging laundry on the line that ran from our house to the garage. Catching my breath, I said, "Mom, I really need to know something about Dad. I heard him crying last night. What is a prisoner of war?" Slowly my mom turned from the clothesline and bent down to my level to look me in the eyes. She never did this unless it was something really important, like she was going to scold me or tell me about somebody who was sick or had died. "Yes, your father was a prisoner of war. It is hard for him, and sometimes he has nightmares reliving what he went through," she said. "He will not talk about it, and I hope you don't ask him about it because it is too painful." She explained that my dad had fought to keep America free at a personal cost to himself, and that this is what happens in war. "Someday perhaps he will tell you his story," she continued, "but for now it is only with him."

This was the last conversation I had with my mom about the war until 1994, after my father died. Over time, I came to understand that my dad's secret was a horrific war experience permanently embedded in his brain. I also understood that his story differed greatly from the war stories of my childhood friends' fathers.

What made my dad different, I wondered. My pals often boasted about their dads' battles and guns. They talked about bombs and Nazis with great excitement. Where did they get these stories? When I asked my dad about his time in the war, he always said the same thing: "Robert, it is not important for you to know."

I often noticed odd things about my dad's behavior. He avoided large crowds or loud and intense events. He wouldn't take my mom on a cruise ship, or let me buy the old army jeep I was offered a good deal on when I was a teenager. We had neighbors with a cyclone steel fence, and my dad was reluctant to enter their backyard. I remember once being outside in our yard with my dad when a large plane flew low over us on its approach to nearby Willow Run Airport. He immediately hit the ground, with no explanation.

Only one time in my life did I attend a major event with my dad that included large crowds and loud noises. I was eight when my family went to the annual Fourth of July fireworks display on the Detroit River. Before she died, my mom recalled that night for me. She and my dad had planned to go to the fireworks with a group of friends and their kids. She said my dad had pressed hard to stay home, but she prevailed upon him to go. I remember my dad trying hard to have fun, but as soon as the fireworks began he grew nervous, edgy, and claustrophobic—he was miserable. His face in the light from the explosions displayed pain and despair. I could tell he wanted to get as far away as possible from the Detroit River. Once the fireworks ended, we left quickly.

I now realize, after talking with my mother and doing my own research, that my dad's behavior that night was the result of his almost daily trips from a Nazi prison camp to Munich during the war. He and other prisoners were stuffed into a cattle train for the three-hour commute to Munich. At the end of the day, they repeated the gruesome ride. If a soldier needed to relieve himself, he was forced to go in an overflowing barrel in the corner. A bad stench, coupled with humiliation and despair, hovered over the railroad car on every trip.

Often Allied bombs rained down on the train as it traveled to Munich. My father's train suffered a direct hit only once. After that disaster, the Nazis realized that painting the letters "POW" in white on top of the boxcar, like a white flag or a red cross, spared the train from a direct bombing. The Nazis weren't worried about the POWs; they were protecting themselves.

Once in Munich, where the POWs worked clearing rubble, they were open targets for American bombs. I can only imagine the horror my father must have felt at the irony of having become the inadvertent target of American bombs meant for the Nazis. The look on his face surely would have been the same one I saw the night of the fireworks.

My dad wouldn't watch war movies. When my uncle asked him if he liked the hit TV show *Hogan's Heroes*, my dad just walked away. My mother told me that the show made him incredibly sad; he believed it mocked the reality of a POW camp. We never watched *Hogan's Heroes* at our house when I was growing up.

I am a baby boomer, born in 1954. Almost every dad in the Dearborn, Michigan, neighborhood where I grew up was a World War II Veteran. My friends and I often overheard the dads in the neighborhood having over-the-fence discussions about their war experiences. This never happened with my dad. He avoided those conversations at all costs. Our neighborhood war games were never played at my house. Everyone in the neighborhood knew my house was off limits. My dad did not like war and would not tolerate me emulating it within his line of sight. I quickly grew to respect his request. We played in other kids' yards, far away from mine.

I never compromised my dad's secret about his POW life. I never told my friends that my dad was cooler than their dads because he had been a prisoner of war. But I cherished knowing that my dad had the best story of all, even though I had no real idea what war was about or how being a prisoner of war might affect someone's body, mind, and spirit.

Of all my childhood memories of my dad, and of his unusual behavior surrounding his war experiences, the episode that stands out the most in my mind is the story of our white picket fence. Dearborn had an ordinance that required residents to fence their backyards along the property lines. The city specified a preference for a cyclone fence. But within a year of moving into our house in 1954, my father had made and erected a white picket fence around our backyard.

Our house on Venice Street was one of the first in Dearborn to have a white picket fence. It was a beautiful fence, each picket hand cut from clear board stock without any knots. Its supporting poles had been cut from an oak tree and individually shaped with a German Peeler. The nail positions were identically placed on each picket and, when painted, formed a graceful white dotted line along the fence. Our fence had four gates, carefully fashioned with oversized hinges, allowing access to our front yard and to the yards of three adjacent neighbors.

We were the only family in our neighborhood with four gates in our backyard fence. It was impossible to be trapped inside our backyard, because a clear exit was visible from every vantage point. My dad needed to know that he could come and go in any direction whenever he pleased.

The significance of this fence to me was its beauty and uniqueness and that my father had made it by hand. Later, when I drilled deeper into my father's war life, I came to see that the white picket fence was directly connected to the nine months he lived as a prisoner of war in 1944 and 1945. For him, it was a way to gain control of something in his life, a way to push back against his unspeakable POW experiences.

My father refused to put a cyclone fence around our backyard. It reminded him of barbed wire and all the time he had spent looking through it, wondering if he would ever be free again. Dad had lobbied the city of Dearborn hard to rescind the fence ordinance. He would have preferred an ordinance banning all fences. Our nearby neighbors supported him, but his efforts came to no avail. So Dad sprang into action, rallying the neighbors and convincing them to let him build a picket fence.

The neighbors surprised my parents by collecting the money to pay for the fence, presenting them with an envelope. The men were all war veterans, and, although none of them had been POWs, each respected my dad and empathized with the unfortunate circumstances of his war. My parents were deeply touched by the kindness and generosity of their neighbors.

My dad's white picket fence stood as a testament to him for over fifty years, until it was finally replaced. But what the fence represented can't be replaced, just as the white crosses that grace Normandy's graves can never be forgotten, even in the face of the ravages of weather and time. Dad could never escape his past, but building the fence helped him to control and quiet the raw memories that were a permanent part of his life.

I loved my dad and liked being around him because he was always doing something interesting. He treated me with dignity and respect. But he was never openly affectionate. I took note of his "can-do" attitude and his incredible mechanical and electrical aptitude. My dad was a brilliant innovator and problem-solver. But I was not as close to him as I was to my mother. An invisible wall stood between me and my father.

Relishing the excitement of life and cherishing the moment did not come naturally to my dad. He was always moving, never feeling. He reacted awkwardly when someone complimented him. It was even more awkward for him when someone embraced him spontaneously, especially if that person was me. I knew that he loved me; he just didn't know how to show it. My dad suffered in silence, enduring the dulling effect of post-traumatic stress disorder before any medical professional had identified the syndrome. He skated on the surface of life, never digging down deep to examine his experiences or his feelings. This was how my dad survived the rest of his life after the war.

I learned a lot from both of my parents. A contrasting but complementary couple, they gave me a great perspective on life. I took the best from both of them and incorporated it into my life. Unlike my dad, I live my life in touch with my emotions, both good and bad, and reach to catch each moment of life's purpose and meaning.

Despite my dad's tendency to be emotionally distant, he managed to have a fantastic marriage that lasted forty-eight years. My mom was crucial in allowing my dad to resume a normal life after the war. She helped him unwind from his ordeal by offering him unconditional love, support, and understanding. I'm sure they both had to make some major adjustments as they grew their lives together. But because of her, my dad didn't end up a loner or a dysfunctional sad case from his war experiences. Not every soldier came home from World War II to the love and companionship that my father returned to.

Dearborn, Michigan, in the mid-1950s was the perfect place to raise a family. It was small, quaint, and new, its streets lined with postwar cookie-cutter houses. In the late 1940s and into the early 1950s, builders in Dearborn couldn't keep up with the demand for housing from war veterans ready to carve out new lives. My parents purchased their house in 1953 for $11,500, which is currently the going price of a sub-compact car without amenities. That Dearborn was the location of Ford Motor Company World Headquarters added to the success and prosperity of the area by keeping property taxes low.

My sister, Debbie, was born in 1948 and I came along six years later. With the addition of our dog, Snooper, we became the perfect family. My mom was the classic 1950s mom, complete with dress and apron. Strikingly lean and beautiful, she was the envy of all my young friends, who wished their moms looked and acted like mine. I loved having a great-looking mom.

My dad got up every day at 5 a.m. and left for work exactly one hour later. He drove forty-five minutes to the heart of Detroit, where he worked until his retirement as an electrician for a large machine building company, Snyder Tool and Engineering. Because of my father, I excelled at school science projects, and I can remember my dad helping me make a light bulb from scratch that ran off of a battery (I took first place). Debbie learned how to sew from my mom, who was a fantastic seamstress, often making our clothes from scratch. Before I knew it, I was in college.

After college, I began a successful career and married Colleen; together we've raised five wonderful kids. My mom died in 2007, outliving my dad by thirteen years. All I have left now are my memories and my desire to understand my dad better and honor his memory by writing this book about his terrible experiences in World War II.

Although my mom was exceptionally close to my dad, it took her a long time to find out everything that had happened to him. Over many years she learned bits and pieces from him and from the army reunions they began to attend.

In the late 1960s, my dad discovered that his army infantry held yearly reunions. I went to three with him, the first one in 1968, when I was fourteen. He'd discuss the war with his fellow 30th Infantry buddies but never his POW experiences. He'd acknowledge that he had been a POW, but no details followed.

My wife, Colleen, and I traveled with our youngest son, Patrick, and our older son, Robbie, to France in March 2008 to visit some of the areas where my dad suffered harshly in the war. We visited Caen, Omaha Beach, and Mortain. The sense of history and awe we felt visiting these haunted places is indescribable. We took photos and saw firsthand where American soldiers had drawn their last breaths. I've made this trip by myself ten times over the last two years to research this book.

In April 2008, Colleen and I took Patrick to a sparsely attended but vibrant 30th Infantry Division Reunion in Fayetteville, North Carolina. I spoke with men who had known my dad. They agreed that he would only go so far when talking about the war, especially if the discussion turned to Stalag VIIA and his experiences as a POW. It is said that time heals all wounds, but this maxim apparently didn't apply to my dad.

My father went through hell and back, and then lived to tell no one but my mom about it. It is clear that his months at war were the most painful, desperate time of his life. Although he took part in the mass assault on D-Day (Day 5) and three other major battles in France, only a glimmer of this part of his war can be found in his writings. My mother told me these battles were gruesome and horrific experiences, but the relentless terror my dad endured in his nine months as a POW greatly overshadowed D-Day and the days that immediately followed.

Through talking with my mother, reading my father's Red Cross Diary, researching the history of Stalag VIIA, interviewing survivors, and traveling to England, France, and Germany, I've been able to recreate my father's extraordinary war experiences. I remain amazed that he managed to survive terrible battles and friendly fire from Allied bombers in France; capture by the Germans; a fifty-two-day march into Germany while being cruelly starved; disease and Nazi brutality in an overcrowded POW camp; the perils of daily travel to work in Munich when it was under constant siege by Allied bombs; and, astonishingly, two daring escapes from the camp.

It is a privilege to tell my father's story.

WEST VIRGINIA CHILDHOOD,
GETTING DRAFTED, MEETING ELEANORE

As a young boy growing up in a West Virginia mining town, it never occurred to my father that one day he would be drafted as a soldier in World War II and ultimately end up in the hardest struggle of his young life.

Herbert Henry Miller was born in Wheeling, West Virginia, on August 20, 1922. Dad was the oldest of four; his siblings were Hank Junior, Phyllis, and Marlene. Their parents, Henry "Pappy" Miller and Helen "Mammy" Miller, were lifelong West Virginians. Pappy had a fourth-grade education, although this was not obvious when you talked with him. Enthusiastic, always willing to learn something new, and innovative in his thinking, Pappy had a distinct edge over many more highly educated men. Pappy was honest and fun-loving, and he taught by example and never raised a hand against his children or anyone else. Mammy was the opposite. Strong-minded and less tolerant, she definitely was the family disciplinarian. Together they presided over a strong family unit and gave their kids the skills they would need to be successful in life.

Windsor Heights, where my dad grew up, is just north of Wheeling, and it sits along the Ohio River surrounded by the many coal mines in that region. High hills and winding roads make this area a rugged but beautiful place. Between the years of 1922 and 1928 our country was in the throes of a pre-Depression, with jobs scarce and money tight. This economic slump was called the Black Doom. My dad always associated Windsor Heights with the subsequent Great Depression. Dad was just seven years old when the stock market crashed on October 29, 1929. Pappy's coal-mine job continued despite layoffs in other industries around him. Coal was essential in the bleak economic times to keep hospitals and government buildings open. Pappy was known for his inventions, which often saved the mine time and money. It was one of the reasons he had a stable, long-term job while the world lay in economic devastation around him.

In April 2008, my uncle Hank Miller recalled what times were like when he and my dad were young:

During the Great Depression, Herb and I were not allowed to wear shoes during the summer, for fear of wearing them out. Mammy was always worried that our growth would overtake the wear. The two big problems Mammy was always concerned about were our shoes and clothes. We had one set of each. If replacement shoes were needed, the stores were empty with none to be found. It became a search. If you were lucky enough to find a pair, let alone the right size, the cost was astronomical. So needless to say, we conserved everything. Somehow Mammy made those shoes last several years, despite our growth.

Herb and I were sent to bed earlier during that time because we only had one pair of clothes to wear each day. Mammy would wash them before she went to bed and hang them to dry, so they would be ready for the next day of school. Food was available but the choices were slim. "Every walking chicken is a target," Herb used to say—that was one of his favorite sayings. Everyone during that time endured hardship and prayed for better times to arrive—fast. Being kids, we were aware of the times, but being kids we were quickly distracted from everyday problems with play and school.

Dad graduated from the eighth grade in 1935 at age thirteen. In step with the times, he enrolled in a technical training school to learn a trade and enter the job market. He studied electronics and mechanics at the McKinley Trade School for three years. Like Pappy, Dad was brilliant when it came to electronics and innovation. His can-do spirit, coupled with his hands-on approach, gave Dad a distinct edge in his thirty-year career at Snyder Tool and Engineering.

Times slowly changed for the better. In 1939, when Dad was seventeen, his family was able to purchase land and build a house eighteen miles south of Windsor Heights in Warwood. The $27 monthly payment was an enormous burden at that time for a family of six. Warwood is a small industrial town on the banks of the Ohio River. The area is dotted with small neighborhoods up in the hills, away from the heavy industry below. I can remember visiting my grandparents as a young boy in the 1950s. I recall a distinct sulphur smell from burning coal, and the constant, distant clanging of the ironworks. My Uncle Hank remembered how the house was built into the side of the hill and had a one-car garage:

> Pappy saw no reason why he could not have a two-car garage—no reason whatsoever. Despite not being able to add on to either side of the garage, due to the bulk of the house on the right and property lines on the left, the only recourse was to dig into the rocky hill and create the space for the second car. Hell, we barely had one car that worked, why did we need space for a second? "Workshop!" Pappy declared. So off we dug, Herb and I removing tons of rock to create the space. To this very day the area still stands unsupported. A true testament to the skill of a coal miner, and the can-do-attitude of Pappy.

At age sixteen, Dad began working part-time at Windsor Coal and Power, one of the largest coal mines near Wheeling and the same one where Pappy worked. Using his skills from trade school, Dad was responsible for the replacement of batteries and bulbs for every lantern and for making sure each man had a helmet ready to go every day. After a couple of years, rechargeable batteries came into vogue, and my dad helped design the charging stations with his father.

Dad also drove the ambulance when needed. When the horn sounded loudly outside Windsor Coal and Power, every person in town knew something bad had happened inside the mine. The workers' wives and children would run from their houses, line up along the dirt road, and pray that their husbands or loved ones had not been injured or killed. Coal mining remains one of the most dangerous jobs in America. During the 1930s, mines collapsed frequently. After an accident, Dad put the ambulance into position and awaited the outcome of that day's calamity. Dad told me that he stopped counting the catastrophes. Often many lives were lost, and, not surprisingly, this shook the foundation of the community every time it happened.

On December 7, 1941, the Japanese attacked the United States at Pearl Harbor. With the subsequent declaration of war, our country's greatest nightmare had begun. The U.S. was now at war in the Pacific and in Europe. Congress adjusted the draft age, lowering it to eighteen. This policy change gave my father his ticket out of West Virginia. I'm not sure it was the ticket he'd been hoping for.

In early summer 1942, an envelope from the War Department arrived at 46 Warwood Terrace with Dad's name on it. He was to report for active duty on October 16 at Fort Thomas in Kentucky, along with four close friends in town who had also been called to serve. Based on war records, I determined that Dad's age of twenty placed him in the group of older soldiers.

According to my Uncle Hank, Dad rose early on October 16, packed a few clothes, ate breakfast with his family, said goodbye to everyone, and boarded a special bus in Wheeling headed for Fort Thomas. The goodbyes had been brief. Determined to be strong and supportive, Pappy and Mammy showed little emotion. At that time, it was a scene repeated daily in towns across America.

When Dad arrived at Fort Thomas, he was tested and questioned to determine if he had any special skills. Unfortunately, no immediate openings existed for jobs that would utilize his talents. Dad's four hometown friends found themselves in the same situation, and this is why they ended up together in the 30th Infantry. Later in the war, his friends were placed in other divisions.

After ten days at Fort Thomas, Dad was transferred to Camp Blanding, in Florida. He stayed there for a year, learning advanced training maneuvers that gave him the tools he needed later to survive the trials of combat and imprisonment. Dad found these maneuvers both exciting and frustrating. Every day his unit was placed in stressful simulated combat conditions. Training in Florida was hard because of the heat and humidity—and the bugs. His stint in Florida was one of the few army experiences my dad ever discussed with me. "The bugs seemed as big as rats, and they often looked scarier than they actually were," he told me.

As dad was in training in Florida, the situation in the Pacific was becoming more grave. In Europe, the war was also escalating. During his sojourn at Camp Blanding, Dad's conversations with his parents revolved around where he would ultimately be sent once he completed his training. Would he be sent to Europe or to the Pacific? Dad's training ended in early January 1944.

The United States military was secretly planning an assault, to be carried out later that year in Europe, that would forever change the direction of the war. Meanwhile, my father returned to Wheeling on furlough and was reunited with his family and friends.

―――――――――――

My mother, Eleanore Helen Kurowski, was born in Detroit in 1922, the same year as my father. My grandparents were Polish immigrants, and Eleanore was the oldest of their five children. The family lived in a duplex, which my grandfather owned, at 7333 Wetherby in the heart of Detroit. The Depression had hit their family hard—my grandfather had lost his job and food was in short supply. But despite the tough times, my grandfather managed to hold on to their house with the income they received from upstairs renters.

My very focused mother refused to let anything get in the way of the plans she'd formulated for her life. A goal-setter, she had as her greatest strength was the ability to keep moving forward whatever the situation. The day after she graduated from high school, my mom got a job at General Dynamics. Eleanore was hired over hundreds of other applicants who'd applied for the same position. Back home she amazed everyone when she walked into the kitchen and announced, "I'm employed." Her father was uncharacteristically speechless. Nobody could believe it.

By 1943 times were still hard in the Kurowski family. Sometimes Eleanore's paycheck was needed to help support the family of seven while her father looked for work. Eleanore was becoming more independent and confident, and she yearned for something better than living with her parents in Detroit.

My mom and dad met at this time. Eleanore had traveled down to Wheeling with Tilley Dunbek, a close friend from work, to meet Tilley's family and friends. Ignoring my grandfather's disapproval, the two girls jumped into a car and drove six hours to Wheeling. A big family reunion was the excitement for the coming weekend. My dad was one of Tilley's cousins.

A strikingly beautiful woman with a warm smile and a soft voice, Eleanore instantly caught the full attention of my father. A member of my dad's family told me: "Your dad immediately took notice when your mom walked in the room. Time basically stopped for Herbert." Despite their initial attraction, though, both assumed the relationship was hopeless. Herbert was in the army, and Wheeling, his hometown, was a long way from Detroit. Herbert told her he expected to be deployed overseas. But they spent the entire weekend together and exchanged addresses so they could correspond. By the time she set off with Tilley for the return trip to Detroit, Eleanore was smitten with the soldier from West Virginia. Herbert was equally smitten and couldn't get the beautiful girl from Detroit out of his mind.

My dad was now on notice that he would be deployed to the European theater in February 1944. The letters started flying between him and Eleanore, sometimes at a rate of two a day. On October 1, 1943, Dad was transferred to Camp Forest in Tennessee, where he stayed for a month. From there he was moved to Camp Atterbury, in Indiana, a drivable distance from Wheeling. Often he was able to get home to Wheeling for weekend visits with his family. He also spent several more weekends with my mom during that time. Love was blossoming between them.

Eleanore gave Herbert two photos of her to take with him overseas. He kept the smaller of the two securely attached by tape to the inside of his undershirt. He carried this photo with him throughout the war, returning home with it intact. After their last visit together in December 1943, Eleanore would not physically see Herbert again for eighteen months. Her picture provided him with tremendous emotional support in the hard months to come.

DAD GOES OFF TO WAR

Early on the cold morning of February 1, 1944, my dad boarded a train bound for Camp Miles Standish, in Boston. Once he was in Boston, discussions in the barracks revolved around what the European war would be like. Most of the young men had never ventured far from their hometowns, and none had any real clue about what to expect, about what they would personally encounter in the coming months.

On the evening of February 12, Dad and his fellow soldiers were ordered to repack their belongings and prepare to board one of the many cruise ships now being used by the military to transport soldiers. He was assigned to the *SS Argentina*, and a young woman from the Red Cross walked up the gangplank with him to bid him farewell. Many of the soldiers were wondering if they might never return home again. The soldiers referred to this fear as "gangplank fever." The trip was a rough crossing, with fierce storms and high waves. Many soldiers suffered from seasickness and attacks from German submarines were a constant threat. After ten tough days at sea, the ship came into port in Gourock, Scotland.

On this trip, the *SS Argentina* had been part of the largest convoy of U.S. troops ever to cross the Atlantic. Each ship was fully loaded, bringing massive supplies and numbers of men to Great Britain. It was common knowledge that Hitler's grip on Europe would not be broken until Allied forces crossed the English Channel to invade France and drive the Germans out. In preparation, a massive build-up was proceeding in Scotland and England.

Dad arrived in Scotland on February 22; two days later he and his company boarded a train and traveled twenty-four miles inland to the city of Glasgow to make room for the troops and supplies continuing to stream into Scotland. The streets of Gourock and Glasgow were teeming with Americans. After seven days in Glasgow, Dad was moved to the port of Bognor Regis, England. From there his infantry unit was transferred to Warminster, England.

The U.S. Army had most of its strength now positioned in Scotland and England. Dad left Warminster by train and traveled in the safety of the night, arriving in Woodbury late in the afternoon on April 6. He would stay in Woodbury until June 8. At night he and his company could hear the howl of air-raid sirens in a distant city. The distinct rough noise of deeply growling airplane engines clearly stood out to them as German aircraft flying inland from the coast. American and British aircraft had a much softer and smoother sound; it did not take long to determine when the enemy was flying nearby. The Germans came close enough to land to let everyone know they were there, but stayed far enough out to avoid being fired on.

It was now clear that something really big was developing and that it would happen in early June. Rumors flew among the soldiers but no one learned the details until a few hours before the event. Uncertainty prevailed, but every soldier knew the massive buildup was for real.

OMAHA BEACH

"The eyes of the world are upon you. . . . I have full confidence in your courage, devotion to duty, and skill in battle."

General Dwight D. Eisenhower, Supreme Allied Commander

T he weather on June 6, 1944, was a bit better than horrific, with unusually strong spring storms in England and on the coast of France. These storms had been assailing the coast for almost a week, and they showed no sign of letting up. High winds, rain, fog, gray skies, and heavy seas pounded the area.

A successful assault on the beaches of Normandy depended on the timing of the new moon, which would enable the Allies to cope with the extreme tides common in the area and expose any underwater obstacles put in place by the Germans. The window of opportunity ended on June 6. The next opportunity would come in two weeks, with the next full moon. But General Eisenhower's advisors believed that it would be half as likely that the conditions would be acceptable in two weeks. And delaying the invasion beyond June would prevent the Allies from gaining the upper hand over the Germans before winter.

Concluding that the weather was not going to cooperate, General Eisenhower in the early morning hours of June 5 reluctantly issued this statement: "Okay, we'll go." The next day, June 6, would be the now-famous D-Day. The Germans did not believe the Allies would be foolish enough to launch an attack in bad weather. The element of surprise was on the Allies' side.

Once Eisenhower gave the order, the mightiest amphibious invasion in history began cutting its way through the waters around the United Kingdom. It was an armada of 5,000 ships carrying 130,000 men and 20,000 vehicles supported by the gunfire of 700 warships, including six monstrous battleships. In addition, 8,000 aircraft were taking part in the effort. The armada was to converge at first light along beaches extending from Cotentin Peninsula on the west to Caen on the east, a stretch of fifty miles.

The true start of the invasion of Omaha Beach was at 2:30 on the morning of June 6, 1944, when the American Airborne Division parachuted into Normandy to secure critical areas near Ste-Mere-Eglise. This town became famous after the 1962 movie *The Longest Day* depicted a parachutist from the 82nd Airborne becoming snagged on the town's church tower during his drop. The massive main invasion started precisely at dawn.

That morning, my dad and his soldier buddies were told of the invasion. They were quickly mobilized, moving to Bournemouth, England, for deployment to Omaha Beach on June 11, 1944.

Omaha Beach was the code name for one of the principal landing points of the Allied invasion of German-occupied France. The five-mile-long beach was located on the northern coast of France, facing the English Channel. U.S. Army troops were given the responsibility of taking the beach, along with U. S. Navy sea transports and a contingent from the British Royal Navy. Little went as planned at Omaha on June 6. Navigation difficulties caused the majority of landing craft to miss their targets throughout the day. The German defenses were unexpectedly strong, inflicting heavy casualties on U.S. troops as they landed.

───────

John McGuckin was my wife's uncle. Colleen had visited him in the hospital during his last illness and learned he'd been on Omaha Beach on

D-Day. McGuckin had been just seventeen years old when he lied about his age and joined the navy. One year later, at eighteen, he was a trained navy seaman, ready for combat. His training enabled him to operate an LCI (Landing Crafts Infantry) on D-Day, carrying personnel and ammunition destined for the war effort against Germany.

I went to see McGuckin after Colleen told me he had been on Omaha Beach. Three days before his death, on June 5, 2008, he told me the following story about what happened to him there. He died one day before the sixty-fourth anniversary of the D-Day invasion.

Under gray skies, and in swelling seas, McGuckin increased his grip on the LCI's helm, mustering all his strength. He quickly put his entire body weight into turning the LCI, pointing it directly into the giant wave about to crash against it. McGuckin's confidence, coupled with his quick reflexes and extensive training, allowed him to skillfully maneuver the LCI in the perilous weather. But sustained high winds off the Normandy coast pushed the swells and waves to greater heights, hampering McGuckin's view of the surrounding area. Glancing from side to side, he could not help noticing that some of the thirty or so soldiers assigned to his boat were feeling the full effects of seasickness. As his eyes scanned individual faces, he realized that in addition to the seasickness many of the men were paralyzed with fear and some were softly crying.

Suddenly Omaha Beach became fully visible to McGuckin. Squinting as he wiped the rain and seawater from his eyes, he could just make out the mass of boats, tanks, men, gunfire, and planes all heading for the coast. But his boat pitched violently, and, instead of the beach, he saw endless gray seawater and frothy white foam. McGuckin knew he was in the pit of the wave and needed to use all of his energy to regain control of his craft to keep it from capsizing. The bone-chilling waves engulfed the men. This scene repeated itself many times before the LCI finally crashed ashore on Omaha Beach.

McGuckin's assignment on June 6 was to make numerous round-trips transporting troops and vehicles to support the D-Day effort. But nothing in his training had prepared him for the sea conditions he was encountering. Avoiding the obstacle course the Germans had placed in the surf was also a major challenge.

As the bottom of the boat finally scraped against the sand on Mc-Guckin's first trip, the men prepared to move out. With gunfire exploding around them, heads were low inside the boat. The LCI landed, and McGuckin committed each soldier to war. He lowered the front gate of his craft, sending the soldiers to hell. Suddenly a young soldier panicked wildly as the troops around him began to push their way off the LCI. Confusion reigned as bullets ricocheted through the air. Some of the men had moved past McGuckin and were still on the ramp when they were hit by shrapnel and bullets and fell face down into the rolling surf. John quickly assessed the young soldier who had panicked, realizing he didn't have a gas mask. Without hesitation, he quickly grabbed his own mask and gave it to the soldier, telling him "God bless you."

Later, I had heard other stories about McGuckin's heroic actions in the war. In the eleven days he spent on the shores of Omaha, he often put his own life at stake to leap out of the LCI and pull wounded soldiers out of the surf, enabling them to survive.

After doing some research, I determined that McGuckin ferried soldiers from the 30th Infantry Division. It is entirely possible that my dad and Colleen's uncle met up in his LCI on June 11. When Colleen was visiting her Uncle Johnny in the hospital, he asked about our recent trip to France. She told him that my dad had been a prisoner of war in World War II. She explained that we'd been trying to trace his steps after he landed on Omaha Beach until the time he was captured by the Germans. When her uncle told Colleen that he had been there on Day One at Omaha Beach, she replied, "That must have been really hard. What was it like?" His eyes welled with tears. "Ah, it wasn't so bad," he said. "Those army guys, they had it real rough."

Stepping off his LCI on the shores of Omaha Beach was a humbling experience for my father. It was not the first time he had witnessed the horrors of death. Back in West Virginia, he had driven an ambulance and picked up bodies after gruesome multiple deaths in coal mine accidents. Dad thought he was mentally ready to handle the war experience. But after landing on Omaha Beach, he realized that the farther he traveled from the sea, the worse things were going to be.

Wading through the chest-deep water, Dad could not help noticing the many shipwrecks protruding from the waves and scattered on the beach. Occasionally an enemy shell would stray from its intended target and explode nearby. His company slowly made its way up the sand dunes, observing the carnage and destruction that were the aftermath of a great battle. On the beach, holes created by the massive artillery shells were large enough for several men to comfortably fit into.

My father had told my mother about landing on Omaha Beach. I heard this story from her:

As your father walked, he could not help noticing the aftermath of war scattered everywhere in the sand. Spent bullet casings littered the landscape and reflected brightly in the sun. Your father mentioned that some of the soldiers joked about how they looked like "jewels in the sand" as they walked on the beach for the first time. They all stopped making jokes as the reality of the situation set in. Your dad felt the severity of war stinging his heart for the first time.

Your dad's heart was heavy with sadness. He felt sick to his stomach, and fear gripped his mind as he silently wondered what each man had experienced on June 6 as his life came to an end. Did they know their lives were ending? Or did it happen so fast they never knew what hit them? As he moved farther inland, your dad's thoughts went even deeper. Would he survive this war? He mentioned that he knew most of the men marching were thinking and feeling the same thing. How could they not?

Having a relationship with someone special gave your dad hope and a reason to be safe. His thoughts were centered on me, and he often looked at the picture of me I had given him. One of his main thoughts was always imagining the war over, him on the boat coming back to America, and seeing me on the dock ready to greet him.

I asked my mom if she was in love with him at that time. She paused for a moment before replying, "Yes, very much." Her face grew red and a tear slid down her face. "Your dad and I were already very much in love, and we could not wait to be together again," she said. "The strain of war was real hard on both of us. But during that time young couples everywhere had the same experience if their loved one was serving in the armed forces. All of us prayed we could be together again. I am the lucky one. Herbert lived to return home to me. I had some girlfriends who were not so lucky."

My mother shared many valuable insights about my dad. She continued, telling me how my father's mind had been constantly gripped with fear:

> Your father didn't know at any moment during the war what his fate might be. It could change at any time. We all live our everyday lives with the uncertainly of not knowing what could happen next. But being in the middle of war greatly increases your risk of death. Compared to you walking down the street in America, the risk is not the same. Your father lost many war buddies he relied on physically and emotionally. Can you imagine how that must feel—living every day with the uncertainty of death hovering at your door?

My dad tried to not think too hard about anything, pushing thoughts of death and other "what ifs" out of his mind. As the infantrymen walked farther inland, the distant sounds of gunfire grew louder and the sounds of the surf on the beach more distant. Dad walked by the tattered fragments of war uniforms on the beach. Some were stained with dried blood and encrusted with sand.

In other secluded areas he observed sand mixed with human blood. This evidence of the destruction of human life troubled my dad, reminding him of the ultimate sacrifice of war. As a boy my dad had hunted with his brother Hank, and they often looked for blood on the ground as they tracked rabbits. But on Omaha Beach the dried dark spots were human blood.

The beach master and his crews had faced the formidable task of claiming the dead, of identifying and burying the thousands of soldiers' bodies. When a body was discovered, it was carefully ticketed with information about that soldier and then readied for burial. Omaha Beach is vast, and finding every component of human remains was a daunting task. Bombs, land mines, and heavy artillery showed no mercy for a soldier who happened to be in their path. The recovery crews worked hard, but it was not possible to clear all the evidence of the great battle in five days time. The sands of Omaha Beach were forever scarred.

The men of the 30th Infantry Division grew quieter as they walked away from the shore. The reality of war and its aftermath was only the beginning of things to come for them. Shock combined with fear in each of these young soldiers. None let on that they were scared as hell, and the march continued.

NORMANDY AND HEDGEROW COUNTRY

After the initial shock of Omaha Beach, the 120th Regiment of the 30th Infantry quickly picked up its pace, continuing to move inland toward the small town of Isigny. After arriving there, the regiment immediately started preparing for contact with the enemy. The men stocked up on food and cigarettes at the canteen. Dad's group relieved the 101st Airborne Division and a part of the 28th Infantry Division. Battle plans were being finalized for the first major attack on the Germans.

The first night, June 11, was incredibly dark, with no moon. To the west, in the area of Omaha Beach, an unsteady quietness prevailed. This was a sharp contrast to what had been going on only five days earlier. To the distant east the fireworks of war illuminated the night sky. The American soldiers could hear the low thunderous explosions of the falling bombs. Everyone knew they were getting very close to the front lines of battle. My dad had not had much sleep in the previous forty-eight hours and was exhausted. Along with the others, he tried to catch some much-needed shut-eye. But the time for sleep didn't last long. Soon the regiment was headed for the front lines. Onward they marched.

As the regiment approached its destination, the soldiers heard the unmistakable sound of a German plane close by. They crossed a small bridge, and the plane dropped a flare over the regiment, instantly lighting up the entire area and exposing its location on the bridge. In a matter of seconds the enemy plane turned and took its aim. The terrible whine of the now nose-diving enemy plane grew closer as it swooped down, dropping several bombs. Dad's group scattered, taking cover wherever they could to escape the blast. Luckily the bombs missed their intended targets.

———

By day Normandy is one beautiful place, with hedgerows dotting the countryside. But the U. S. Army never anticipated the need to provide training to its soldiers about how to penetrate and fight within hedgerows. In medieval times, hedgerows were built along property lines and roads. Composed of rocks and debris picked up during plowing, hedgerows were placed along the perimeter of each field. Through the centuries, trees and thick bushes started to grow in them, and hedgerows became nearly impenetrable. Many of the oldest are almost fifteen feet high.

After the D-Day invasion, U.S. army engineers made ingenious use of the hundreds of metal beach blockades the Germans had placed in the sand at Omaha Beach to stop the LCIs from coming ashore. The engineers cut them up and welded makeshift punching blades onto the American tanks. The army quickly discovered that they could use the tanks equipped with the punching blades, along with dynamite, to obtain quick passage through hedgerows.

Often after Dad's regiment rammed a passage through a hedgerow, the Germans were on the other side waiting to pick off soldiers. Many soldiers died trying to pass from field to field. My father lost several buddies while fighting in hedgerows, which offered no advantages to the Allies. The Allies were knocking on the Germans' door.

My father often commented to my mother on the unique smell of Normandy. This included the odor of Cordite, a smokeless explosive powder made of nitrocellulose, nitroglycerin, and petrolatum that had been dissolved in acetone, dried, and extruded in cords. The Cordite stench blended with the fragrance of crushed apples and hundreds of rotting cattle to create the distinct smell of 1944 Normandy. I heard my father refer to what he called "reminder smells," especially when he was at one of my uncle's farms in Michigan. I remember the look in his eyes and how differently he acted when something reminded him of the smell of Normandy.

———————

Fighting steadily increased in the weeks after my dad landed in Normandy. The process of gaining ground against the Nazis was slow and arduous. Most of the soldiers were becoming sleep deprived, because contact with the enemy was a twenty-four-hour affair. Catnaps gave the men a mental break from the war, but they never lasted long enough. A sleeping soldier would be jolted back to reality when bombs or grenades exploded close by. When I was a kid on my way to summer camp, my dad would tell me that he used to "pull up a rock, and use it as a pillow." I never believed him for a minute back then, but I do now.

As June progressed, battles became daily events. Making progress through the hedgerows was difficult, slow, and dangerous. Sometimes my father's group would be only fifty feet from the Germans, with everyone in their respective foxholes. They could not talk or move freely about without being discovered. Commonly the Americans would be separated from the Germans by only a fifteen-foot hedgerow. A stalemate would ensue until one side decided to break through and strike out at the other.

The army taught soldiers to dig two types of holes. The traditional foxhole, essential for a soldier's survival, was for longer stays; the slit trench was a quick fix for one-night stands. In rainy Normandy, the foxholes were frequently wet and muddy, but the soldiers welcomed them when darkness fell or the action of battle became too intense.

The 30th Infantry did not have access to hot showers from the time they left for Normandy on June 10 until late July. In hedgerow country there were no showers, bathrooms, or hot meals available. Dad lived off his C- and K-rations, which provided him with enough calories to do his job. C-rations consisted of three cans per day per man, and K-rations

Michigan Hedgerows

When I was a child, I knew about hedgerows. Two of my uncles owned farms in southern Michigan, which we often visited. Several of the smaller fields were bordered by hedgerows, although they weren't nearly as large as Normandy's hedgerows. As a child, I loved to be out in the pasture playing and exploring the fields surrounded by the high dirt walls of the hedgerows. Climbing up on one of them was like climbing a mountain, I thought. I liked the unsteady feeling when I arrived at the top, often out of breath.

My uncles' farms were well-established and located in rolling Michigan countryside; the original owners had, like the French, piled up rocks and debris from the fields to make the hedgerows. According to my mother, and my own memories, my father did not like venturing into rolling fields that were small and confining, especially if the field was surrounded with barbed-wire fencing. I can recall Dad going out of his way to avoid entering my uncles' fields. He always had a good excuse. I never gave it a thought when I was young.

I remember one Saturday in early June when we visited one of my uncle's farms for the weekend. It was hot and dry and the smell of freshly plowed fields still lingered in the air. I asked my dad to take me fishing. He hesitated, but agreed. You see, the pond was on the other side of the hedgerow field, and either you had to walk through this field or drive to the pond on the dirt road, which took twice as long. I was a typical impatient kid who wanted to get wherever I was going quickly. My choice was to walk and explore. Dad's choice was to drive the car around the longer way, avoiding the small, confining field, and this is what we did.

My dad's fears were subtle but real. It makes me sad to think of the emotional burden he carried throughout his postwar life. He tried to cover up his fears, especially when I was a child. I recall a man who often didn't seem to have a care in the world. But when he was pressed to participate in everyday events that reminded him of his past, the nightmare that had been his war returned.

were three boxes of a variety of concentrated foods. A soldier needed 40 percent more food than normal to keep him going during the war. My guess is that my dad was always starving, because I remember he liked to eat a lot.

THE WOODEN SHOES

On the morning of June 21, 1944, my father's emotional health suffered its first devastating blow. Tragedy would now cruelly take center stage, leaving him awash in sadness and despair.

During my childhood a pair of hand-carved wooden shoes in the size of a six- or seven-year-old child was on display in our upstairs bookcase. Close inspection revealed soil stains and the wear and tear from having been worn by a young child. Steel nails were affixed to the bottom of the shoes. To me they were just a pair of wooden shoes. But when I would put them on and parade around our upstairs floors, I was promptly ordered to take them off. My father had carved on one of the shoes the following inscription: "France June 21, 1944."

I heard the story of the shoes from my mother many years later. My dad's regiment was dug in, camping near a small French farm away from the front lines of battle. The 30th was getting some much-needed rest, but they were still involved in active fighting. Every morning and evening my father and several other soldiers would travel to the tiny farm, which had a working well. They always took the time to visit with the family that owned the farm: a mom and dad and their four little girls between the ages of two and twelve.

My father was a leader in his group, and he made the decision to frequent this farm and to use their water supply. Gaining trust was an essential element on both sides. Soon the family graciously welcomed ather and his group every day. They were grateful, they said, that the Americans were liberating France. Even with the language barrier, the soldiers and the French family communicated well.

I can imagine that my father's warm smile and friendly personality helped gain this family's confidence. At every visit the American soldiers surprised the children with candy and chewing gum. The six-year-old daughter took an instant shine to my father. He would lift her up onto his shoulders and sing to her as he paraded around. My mother told me that the little girl would laugh with glee, and her sisters would join in the fun. The parents were so happy to see joy and excitement returning to the lives of their girls. The family treated my dad and his group like heroes, because they offered hope, love, and friendship during the bleakest of times.

All the hope and promise for this family came to an end in the early morning hours of June 21. Late one night, almost forty years to the day after it happened, my father awakened tearful from another nightmare and finally decided to tell my mother how the story of the French family had ended. These are his words, as told to me by my mother:

We did not get much sleep the night of June 20 due to higher-than-normal activity. Gunfire, planes, and tank movement by the Nazis were increasing throughout the night. Somehow I fell asleep for a time. I woke suddenly around four to darkness and an unusual silence. The fog was present in the lower valleys, and that had most likely calmed the movement of the Germans. We quickly pulled together our group and the supplies we needed and proceeded to the farm for water. The sun was coming up. We traveled cautiously through the fields, always expecting some run-in with the Nazis. Ironically, for the last several days we'd been free of them.

As we came close to the farm, we expected the children to be up and ready for our visit; they always looked forward to it. Approaching the farm, we noticed an unusual silence and the absence of the roosters or chickens that were always in the yard. Instantly we knew something was horribly wrong. We readied our guns and carefully approached the house. It was terrible. Our hearts were beating out of our chests. We approached the door of the house to knock but discovered it un-latched and open. All of us knew this was not a good sign. We quickly went into the house with our guns drawn and searched each room. To our amazement, the house was intact with nothing missing. We retreated and moved to search the barn behind the house. We entered the barn and discovered the entire family shot dead.

The bodies of the family, shot execution-style, were in the back stall of the barn where the now-missing cow had lived. The Nazis had de-cided to punish the family for providing food and support to American soldiers. My father told my mother that the Nazis who had done this were of the SS variety. They were ruthless, arrogant, and extremely loyal to Hitler's war machine. Aiding and abetting the enemy meant certain and immediate death with no questions.

Shaken to the core, my dad and his group cried as they prepared to bury their friends. One of the distraught men discharged his weapon wildly into a nearby tree. My dad noticed that even under duress the family had taken the time to slip on the wooden shoes they wore to work in the fields and walk to the barn. Perhaps they never understood what was going to happen to them.

As they buried the family on their farm, Dad carefully slipped off the wooden shoes from the special girl, the one he always gave his shoul-der rides to, and placed them in his pack. After the burial, they tossed grenades into the house and barn, making sure it was uninhabitable to the Germans. They returned to their regiment for another day of war, all expected to function normally despite the mind-numbing sadness each of them felt. My father's heart was ripped from his chest that day, but this was only the beginning of Herbert Miller's war.

My dad immediately sent the little girl's wooden shoes home to his parents. Years later, when I asked my father about the shoes in our bookcase, he replied in his usual kind way: "They were from a farm in France."

ST. LO AND OPERATION COBRA

Returning to the front line of fighting in early July, my dad's regiment walked right into a major counterattack. The Germans hit them with all they had, breaking through their defenses and penetrating their lines. Fighting back furiously, the regiment somehow maintained their hold despite suffering severe damage to their defenses and loss of life within the ranks. Finally, most of the fighting stopped, and it was now time to move out. Dad was in the first of eight jeeps in the convoy. He told my mother this story:

> As we pulled out from our last position, we carefully started driving down this dirt road that had been cut open by German Panzers days before. We all understood that even if the direct fighting had stopped, there was always a risk of German snipers in the area. Suddenly, out of nowhere, snipers started shooting at us. Bullets were bouncing off of jeeps—all we could hear were gunfire and pings.
>
> Several of the jeeps behind me took the brunt of the gunfire. Some of our men were hit very badly, and those jeeps just stopped in their tracks. It was my instinct and training to get the hell out and fast, so I pushed the accelerator to the floor and discovered that my engine was no longer working. I pulled my pistol from my belt, dove to the

41

ground, firing my gun all the way, and then rolled under the jeep for cover. I couldn't believe I hadn't been hit. After a few seconds, the remainder of our company arrived and pumped so many bullets into the areas where the snipers had been firing from that it wasn't long before all of them were killed.

We somehow regained our composures, but had now lost another six men from sniper fire. It was real sad. I figured, OK I'm lucky, thank God, but my confidence had now vanished. I was immediately ordered to go back to the motor pool for another jeep. Petrified at the thought of having to go back through the woods again, I somehow managed to get back to the motor pool area and pick up another jeep. This time I found a mechanic and took him with me. I figured I might need him in the future, in case I developed more jeep trouble.

I was now real scared and jumpy all the time. Every time I heard sniper fire after that episode, out came my fifty-caliber submachine gun, and I was looking for that sniper bastard. If I found him, I was going to cut him to ribbons. It was either the Thompson or I'd jump for the fifty-caliber, because I was determined after experiencing sniper fire that I was never going to die from that or lose another jeep.

─────────

Fighting with the Germans was a surreal experience. They left their individual marks of death and destruction. I overheard my father telling my Uncle Mike this story many years ago: Dad remembered how the Nazis booby-trapped anything they left behind. They knew the Americans were souvenir hunters and collectors, and they made good use of this knowledge.

Often the Nazis would covertly attach a very thin piano wire to an item they thought would be of interest to an American. Common examples were food, wine, or even dead bodies. The wire was carefully concealed within the debris or buried in the dirt. Approximately two to six feet from the item of interest they'd place a personnel mine, or other type of explosive device, ready to explode once the wire disturbed the firing mechanism. Although trained to spot and avoid these traps, soldiers were often in a hurry and became careless. Some paid a heavy price for their lack of attention to past training. Dad lost several of his buddies this way. These were tragic episodes that eroded his confidence and increased his anxieties as the war progressed.

Another scary tactic the Nazis employed was stringing thin wire, tightly stretched at chest height, between two trees. In the daylight it was almost impossible to see this wire spanning the road. At night, forget it—the wire was impossible to see, and a jeep driver would head right into the trap and be decapitated instantly. My dad worried about this constantly because he drove a jeep most of the time during the war. He recalled how a jeep in front of him became a victim of this gruesome tactic. Fortunately, the windshield had been up and had broken the wire before it could snap the soldier's neck.

The Fourth of July that year was acknowledged but not much celebrated. According to published memoirs of the 30th Infantry, and a story my dad told my mother, when July 4 arrived everyone in the division was told to fire one shot simultaneously. At the appointed moment of 1 a.m., everything from the large 155mm artillery to the smallest pistol was fired in one thunderous bang that echoed throughout the rolling fields of Normandy. It was reported that the Germans had no clue what was going on, and stress and confusion ensued among their ranks.

It took more than sixty days after D-Day for the Allies to move sixty miles from the beachhead. In less than three weeks, a million Allied troops were firmly entrenched on French soil. The liberation of Ste. Mere Eglise, Carentan, and Cherbourg gave the Allies their first major victories in the battle for Normandy. But the cost was horrific, with more than 142,000 causalities on both sides. Winning the war was still a long way off. By early July, the U. S. and its allies stood face to face with German soldiers in a stalemate. If the Germans had continued to successfully hold back our troops, they would certainly have won the war. The

Allies needed an innovative and creative master plan to get them beyond Normandy, and they had to come up with it fast.

St. LO was the first step. Only twenty miles from the landing beaches, it was the crossroads to all other cities in France. The fight for Hill 192, in St. LO, was critical for the Allied effort because it was the highest hill in Normandy. Three days of bloody fighting with three divisions, including Dad's 30th, were part of a struggle to take the high ground, a ridge, just to the west of St. LO. Historical accounts of the Battle of St. LO claim that the 29th Infantry Division fought and won it. However, both the 35th and the 30th Infantry divisions provided major assistance to the 29th. Without the assistance of these dedicated divisions, the battle would have lasted much longer, and resulted in a greater loss of lives for the men of the 29th.

Finally, on July 20, after a bloody battle, St. LO was liberated and placed in the hands of the 29th Infantry. My father and his fellow soldiers in the 30th Infantry successfully removed the Germans from their prime observation spots overlooking St. LO. Without this help, the 29th would not have been able to gain entrance to and liberate the city of St. LO.

Liberation came with a price. General Omar Bradley's First Army had suffered over 40,000 war causalities in just seventeen days of combat. After the battle of St. LO, Bradley needed to quickly move out of hedgerow country. A major offensive was under development, and the plans for it would soon be shared with the troops. As his regiment prepared to move out of Normandy, Dad's own fate would soon be on the line.

———————

Meanwhile, the news quickly spread that Adolf Hitler had barely escaped an assassination attempt by his own generals on July 20. Hitler, who survived with minor injuries, rounded up and ordered killed anyone even remotely involved in the plot against him. To calm his mind, he also ordered the killing of 3,000 German civilians. When word of this reached my father and his division, it only made the men of the 30th more determined to do whatever it was going to take to rid Europe and the world of this madman. Suddenly the war became a new mission for my father. He wanted Hitler dead, and it reignited some of his courage as he pressed on.

The next major task for the Allies was to create a breach in the German defenses that ran parallel to the St. LO—Periers highway. Operation Cobra was under way. The 30th Division's baptism by fire was about to begin, and my dad sensed that his life could be in serious jeopardy. Operation Cobra was of major importance to the success of the war. The Germans were not going to give up easily because the MLR (major line of resistance) was a critical stronghold for all German defenses. The Krauts, as my father called them, were well hidden in the vines, bushes, and trees, and they had dug in solidly in the ground. They were well positioned to defend to the death, as ordered by their leader, Hitler.

Dad's group now had time to reorganize during the lull in fighting. Replacement soldiers were brought in to fill in the spots opened by the many casualties of the past month. My father had lost three of his buddies in the preceding weeks. This misfortune, on top of the massacred French family, was causing him to disengage mentally.

Dad and the other soldiers were resupplied with additional equipment, ammunition, and food in anticipation of the expansion of troop strength after Operation Cobra was completed. My dad told my mother: "The plans and preparations that were being crafted for Operation Cobra were intense. We were told that failure was not an option." Dad's commanders had prepared his group for their individual jobs and made sure they clearly understood the overall objectives and the importance of the mission to the overall war effort. But my dad was silently struggling with his own demons: the uncertainty of the mission's success, his own mortality, and the possibility of massive death and destruction. He told my mother:

Fighting as a soldier in the line of battle doesn't allow you a clear perspective of the overall progress of war. You may be winning battles in your own little circle, but how successful is the overall war effort? Every one of us frequently questioned whether our efforts and sacrifices would help win this war. Would it be enough? I was just so fed up with losing my buddies by sniper, bombs, or gunfire. Some days I just wanted it to all go away. I needed them and they needed me, or so I thought. I remember telling myself more than one time to stop making friends, because the odds were stacked against all of us living. It was mentally easier to stay detached and not get emotionally involved with your fellow soldiers. Any of us could catch a fatal bullet. Sometimes I thought the soldier who was mortally wounded had the emotional advantage, because he never had to deal with the sadness and emptiness again.

I adopted this way of thinking for about one lousy hour. The very minute all hell broke out, and you were in the foxhole fighting and trying to survive, there was no way you could stay detached. The bonds of reliance, gratitude, and joint survival quickly change a person during very stressful times. When you and your buddy narrowly escape death once again, it is hard to not feel some connection with each other, especially if he saved your ass. I can tell you this: If a fellow soldier who I might not know ended up in my foxhole and we fought together for several days, barely escaping death's door together, and then lived to see another day, you can bet we'd be linked together emotionally.

My mother told me this story on August 10, 2005. She remembered it exactly as my father told it to her. She had just moved into her new home in the same city where I live, and this was the longest conversation I ever had with her about my father's war. We spent the better part of an afternoon together uncovering my father's war experiences.

Operation Cobra's target date was now July 24, and H-Hour was set for 11:30 in the morning. The high-ranking officials were in England coordinating the battle plan and attack sequences with the Air Corps. Considerable arguments took place concerning the Air Corps' plan of attack. The Air Corps wanted to bomb head-on the St. LO—Periers highway, which was perpendicular to the German MLR. This plan would limit the exposure time for the planes and make it harder for German anti-aircraft artillery to fire upon the troops.

General Bradley took strong exception to this plan, believing it was too risky and that it would cause bombs to miss their targets. "Every bomb must count," said Bradley. The Air Corps was told to make flight plans to bomb the MLR from east to west, parallel to the St. LO—Periers highway. This would lessen the possibility of any bombs dropping short of their targets and landing directly on our troops. Finally, after many hours of deliberation and disagreement, Bradley and the Air Corps settled on their final plans. Operation Cobra could now begin.

A few hours before the massive strike, the 30th Infantry was pulled back 1,200 yards to the north, to protect them from misdirected bombs or artillery. One hour before the event, more than fifty artillery battalions were firing into the target area. The ground shook violently, and the noise from the explosions was deafening. My mother told me my father's heart had been beating so fast he felt sick to his stomach. Some of his fellow soldiers were so nervous with anticipation that they became sick. Unfortunately, they had to get over it, collect their guts, and be ready to fight. The bombs began to drop, announcing to the Germans the onset of Operation Cobra, the heaviest artillery barrage since the Omaha Beach landings.

The operations included 3,000 airplanes in all, carrying 4,000 tons of explosive power. Bombers from the 8th and 9th Air Corps dropped their bombs parallel to the American lines. Bradley hoped to punch a hole in the German lines for American troops to move through and end the stalemate. The plan was very risky, and, unfortunately, the Air Corps and the army on the ground had very different ideas about what was supposed to happen.

Fifteen minutes prior to the H-Hour, the 30th Division Artillery fired a series of red smoke shells focused on the southern side of the St. LO—Periers highway. Hitting precisely, the red smoke exploded and began to disperse just as planned along the MLR and the highway. The attack had begun, and everything was working perfectly. To continue to make it work as scheduled, the Air Corps needed to fly over the American troops and drop the bombs in front of them. But due to thick clouds and fog in England, Bradley called the mission off at the last minute. Unfortunately, 1,600 planes had already taken off and were quickly heading toward their targets.

The French countryside that day was sunny and bright. A slight breeze came up unexpectedly, and the smoke began to slowly drift back toward the north. In just a matter of minutes, the red smoke was on top of the men of the 30th Infantry, including my father waiting for H-Hour to begin. Panic and confusion overtook the once-confident men, who understood they were now the target and in serious trouble. In less than two minutes, 1,600 planes that had been instructed to fly in "full radio silence" to the end of their mission began dropping 2,000 tons of explosive power directly on top of the 30th Division.

With no ground-to-air liaison or contact, it was impossible to warn the pilots of the northwest drift of the red smoke and order them to stop dropping bombs on American troops. As the armada of air power continued to release its bombs, all planes were focused directly on the red smoke line. My father's instincts told him he was in serious trouble, and he began to pray.

As the bombs landed and exploded, it was every man for himself. My father was with five other men inside a large foxhole that offered some protection. As the carpet of bombs continued to fall, my dad could see them striking their targets ahead of his foxhole. Dad remembered the sound as being like the rapid fire of a machine gun. He could see in the distance many of his fellow soldiers sustaining direct hits inside their foxholes. The men were being vaporized into oblivion.

In instances of extreme stress a human mind can process many thoughts at once. Dad knew by the sound of their engines that the planes flying overhead were American. The bombs continued to explode, coming closer and closer to my dad's foxhole. He remembered somehow losing his gun and quickly taking off all of his ammunition and grenades and tossing them out of the foxhole to prevent a secondary explosion. He eventually found his gun and held on to it for dear life. The men in the foxhole knew that if they were going to survive they'd have to find better cover. Shrapnel, dirt, and debris were flying around them. The cries of men rose above the thunderous explosions. My dad quickly calculated his chances of surviving and decided with the others, all now in a full state of panic, to move to a more secure area rather than waiting for a direct bomb hit. There was nothing they could do, no enemy to fight. All that was left was to pray, react, and hope for the best.

Meanwhile, everywhere in his line of sight my father saw American bombs raining from the sky with increasing intensity. Peering through the thick black smoke, one of the men noticed a ravine next to a big hedgerow near some large trees. The men timed their exodus from the foxhole, waiting for a slight break in the action. They scurried to take cover in the trench between explosions.

Just as Dad arrived at the top of the ravine, a large bomb exploded, sending him flying into one of the large trees. He stretched out his arms and extended his gun, which broke the impact as he hit the tree. Bouncing off, he fell into the muddy water at the bottom of the ravine. Bombs were now falling everywhere around him. Feeling slightly relieved, he looked around for the other men. He saw only two of the five men who'd been with him in his foxhole. Feelings of sadness, confusion, and disbelief overwhelmed him.

Suddenly my dad felt an unfamiliar burning in his upper right thigh. It took a while for him to comprehend that he'd been wounded. The onslaught of bombs continued around him. Still fearing a direct hit, my dad buried his face in the mud and prayed hard to be allowed to survive this living hell. What seemed like hours of bombing suddenly ended. The sounds of the airplanes and exploding bombs ceased. Dead and wounded men who had not even had the opportunity to fight against the enemy were everywhere. How could this tragedy have been allowed to happen?

Once my dad's heart rate returned to normal, he found the courage to look up. He felt the now intense burning in his thigh and glanced back down at his blood coursing through the muddy water. Not able to stand on his wounded leg, he grabbed a tree branch. Pulling himself out of the water, he stood on his good leg to survey the results of the bombing attack. Focusing his attention back on his bad leg, he noticed a piece of shrapnel sticking out of it. His fellow soldiers held on to him tightly to keep him above the water.

Soon a passing medic came to the rescue, instructing the men to lift my dad out of the ravine, place him flat on the ground, and elevate his legs. He was given a shot of morphine, and after a quick examination the shrapnel was removed, the wound cleansed, and sulfa powder placed directly on it. The medic declared Dad's injury bad but not life threatening. With a few quick stitches, he would be as good as new.

Dad was transferred to the regiment aid station, where he received eight stitches and was told to take it easy for the rest of the day. Happy to be alive, he was not evacuated away from the front line and returned to battle the next day.

Among the American regiments under friendly fire that day, the 30th suffered the most casualties. In Dad's regiment thirty men had been killed; another 156 were wounded. His close friends from childhood, the twins Jim and Tim Nodurft, were both killed in Operation Cobra.

The Germans had not retaliated, and their front line remained quiet. American leaders made the tough decision to repeat the same battle plan on the following day, July 25.

Later in the day, my dad and his fellow soldiers went looking for the three men who hadn't made it to the ravine. Heading for the foxhole, they discovered it had sustained a direct hit. They'd gotten out just in time. Their three comrades had decided to stay in the foxhole.

That morning six soldiers woke up, not knowing what that day had in store for each of them. By late morning, quick, instinctive decisions had saved the lives of three of them. The other three, deciding they were safer staying in the foxhole, ended up on the Missing in Action list. They'd been vaporized, and their bodies were never found.

The next morning dawned bright and sunny, just like the day before. Replacement soldiers were brought in to fill in the ranks. Chaos prevailed all around. The misdirected bombs had landed as far back as the regiment headquarters. The hospital, ambulances, and phone lines had all been destroyed. Most of the two-way radios had been damaged, and little or no communication was possible between the regiment headquarters, brigade headquarters, and the companies located near the battlefront. Runners were now traveling between the various command posts to deliver the instructions and messages essential for the second effort to proceed.

Despite having made the commitment to move forward once again, General Bradley was still in shock. Not surprisingly, a major inquiry was under way. Why had the Air Corps dropped bombs perpendicular to the MLR after agreeing to bomb parallel to it? Who was responsible for this change? Confusion and anger reigned. The men of the 30th Division were understandably demoralized. The events of the day before seemed unbelievable to my dad and to everyone else. Today was going to be very different, or so they all thought.

Unknown to most of the soldiers, Lieutenant General Leslie McNair had left his post in Washington D.C. and was assigned to a newly created position based in Europe. On this day he was at the headquarters of the 2nd battalion of the 120th Infantry Regiment. His mission was to observe and gain some understanding of how things had gone so wrong the day before. It was going to be up to him to ensure that the mistakes were not repeated.

Dad and his buddies, who had escaped death the previous day, were still struggling with their emotions. My dad told my mother he was black-and-blue almost everywhere on his body from the impact of hitting the tree. His leg was sore, but he could walk and, if necessary, run on it. He was on edge most of the time and had a constant ringing in his ears from the bomb blast. His buddies from the foxhole were younger than him and filled with fear and questions. Ironically, they looked up to my father as their leader, although they were all ranked as privates first class.

Once again Dad and all the other infantrymen were withdrawn 1,200 yards to the north, in case any bombs or artillery missed their targets and fell short. Many of the soldiers were anxious and stressed after surviving the direct hit from the previous day's mishap. The commanders assured everyone everything was in place for the start of Operation Cobra. The presence of a three-star general ensured that the mission would be completed successfully. Red-smoke shells were fired again, and they landed exactly where they were supposed to along the MLR just south of the St. LO—Periers highway. This time, all 3,000 airplanes carrying 4,000 tons of explosive power were on their way. With the cloudless sky, it was easy to see the low-flying bombers as they approached their target areas.

From the ground Dad could clearly see the bomb doors on all of the planes slowly opening and beginning to drop the first line of bombs. But a disaster was once again in progress. My father, now even farther back from the MLR, looked up from his cover and to his horror observed the previous day's deadly scenario playing out again. The red smoke was once again drifting toward him and all of the 30th Infantry troops. Soon red smoke and bombs were once again intermingling with disastrous results.

My dad was next to a small bridge and a culvert studded with large trees. He quickly said a prayer and, along with the others, smashed his body and face into the mud and hung on for dear life. The bombs rained down like hail in a thunderstorm. Explosions, debris, dirt, and smoke were everywhere. Luckily, this time Dad was in an area that avoided direct bomb drops. He always credited his survival to God's intervention. Until his death fifty-one years later, he remained unable to understand how or why he survived those two days. My mother told me she heard this story from Dad only one time, when he woke up from one of his bad dreams. On this night he let it all out over a pot of coffee with my mother as they stayed up until dawn talking about his horrific war experiences.

The magnitude of the tragedy was impressive, with sixty-four more men killed, 374 wounded, and over sixty missing in action. All were in my dad's division. This time the direct hits on the men led to an increase in the Missing in Action list. Some were buried alive and later accounted for. Some were instantly vaporized and never found.

Since the bombing once again extended back to the regiment head-quarters, General Bradley and other high-ranking officials ran for cover, barely escaping with their lives. General McNair, the three-star general, died that day, becoming the highest-ranking general killed in World War II. McNair suffered a direct hit.

More than 600 American causalities resulted from the two days of misguided bombing. General Bradley and the airmen began pointing fingers at one another. Dad's regiment was suffering from severe battle fatigue. All of the surviving men should have been sent back behind the lines for rest and recovery. The commanders had to decide whether to cancel or go ahead with the attack. The divisions that had not been affected by the errant bombs were ready to participate in the operation. As for the Germans, they had been warned twice about what was to come. Clearly the element of surprise was no longer a factor. The commanders quickly made the decision to proceed with the attack as planned.

The front-line units were hastily reorganized. Replacement soldiers were not available. Every man was going to have to pull his own weight and then some. Now the demoralized and poorly led 30th Infantry was going to have to muster the strength to perform a miracle with the equipment and supplies they had left. The divisions moved forward and attacked. Dad was able to fight despite his bad leg. His stitches broke open, exposing the wound to dirt and infection, but he carried on.

As the Americans advanced, it became clear that the Germans had not sustained much damage from the two days of bombings. Apparently the 30th had sustained more death and destruction than the enemy. The Germans were well dug in and enjoyed good defensive positions. But a flaw existed in the German armor. They were unable to move any armor, heavy artillery, or replacement troops to the front of their lines. This made it relatively easy for the 30th and the other divisions to breach and penetrate the German main line of defense. Once it was opened up, General Patton and his Third Army were able to break through and head for Brest, France. God appeared to be on the side of the 30th and the other divisions.

After successfully penetrating the German lines, the 30th Infantry Division was now sent into reserve for rest and recovery for the first time since their combat action had begun on June 15th. After a horrific stretch of forty-nine days, my dad was finally able to have the now-open wound on his leg re-stitched, take a shower, and eat a warm meal. The USO provided a show, and movies were made available, offering a great change of pace for the men.

The eleven-day battle at St. LO and Operation Cobra had decimated the 30th Division forces. With 3,934 casualties, the division had lost almost 40 percent of its men. The toll among the front-line rifle platoons was even higher, at close to 75 percent. It is amazing that my father survived. A German general, reviewing the carnage around St. LO, called it a "monstrous bloodbath."

Unquestionably, the 30th Infantry Division's valor and determination to succeed against overwhelming odds is a noteworthy and historically important World War II story. After a few days, the rest period was over and the 30th was ordered to move quickly out to the small French city of Mortain, which was critical to the war effort. It was here that my father's journey through the war took a major turn. His life was about to be altered and his spirit forever changed.

MORTAIN

After the 30th Division's successful penetration of the Germans' main line of defense, Adolf Hitler now clearly understood what the U.S. Army was capable of accomplishing. With the completion of Operation Cobra, the German Army was now unraveling at the seams. Operating from his underground command post at Saint Germaine, outside of Paris, German Field Marshall Günter Von Kluge had now become the target of Hitler's rage and fury. There must be no more withdrawals. The German Army must counterattack immediately and close the Avaranches-Mortain corridor, commanded Hitler. He now ordered his army to the sea.

Von Kluge had been completely responsible for the failure of the German Army against Operation Cobra. He knew that any protest to Hitler would be in vain. He also knew that he was about to be confronted with his final opportunity to trap General Patton's Third Army. The twenty-mile-long corridor to Mortain, France, was now the focus and target of the Germans, and their success or failure was going lead to either the rebirth or the beginning of the end of the Third Reich. The key to the entire operation was Mortain. Von Kluge quickly assembled over 400 tanks and many thousands of men, all focusing on the sleepy city. Soon orders would be given to deploy this mass of German might to hold back the Americans and win Mortain.

Meanwhile, my dad's shrapnel wound was not healing well after the second set of stitches he'd received. The wound was now infected, and he had a fever. The medic took one look at my dad's leg and decided to open up the wound again, which was very painful. But because every man was needed for the movement to Mortain, the medic stitched my dad's wound to the maximum to keep it from reopening and becoming reinfected on the battlefield. In retrospect, that medic did a very good thing for my father. After he was captured by the Nazis and marched for 1,300 kilometers across France into Germany, he had no access to any medical assistance whatsoever. If my dad's wound had become reinfected, the Germans would most likely have shot him. The SS showed no mercy when inconvenienced by American soldiers.

On August 4 the 30th Infantry was in Tessy-sur-Vire regrouping and preparing for a battle at Mortain. Late in the day the regiment was alerted that they would be moving out soon. My father's wound was now healing, and he was amazed by how much better he felt. With a large but secure bandage attached to his leg, the soreness was gone and he could move about freely. He was no longer worried about being hampered in battle. This gave my dad a much-needed shot of confidence, despite the perils that were staring him in the face. The next day the 30th Division passed to the control of the VII Corps and was ordered to progressively relieve the 1st Division as soon as possible. My dad's unit was under orders to move out to Mortain.

As the Infantry traveled the forty-five miles toward Mortain, all was calm and uneventful. When they arrived, families lined the roads and cheered, showering the men with flowers and drinks. The people of Mortain were under the delusion that they'd finally been freed of the Germans after their liberation by the 1st Infantry on August 3. Dad and his fellow soldiers relished this experience because it was a huge mental lift. Finally they could see some of the benefits of their hard work over the past sixty days. It was good to encounter families who were feeling whole again and free from Nazi occupation, my father was thinking.

For the first time in many weeks his spirits lifted a bit. The faces of the French families said it all.

Mortain is not much different today from how it was in late summer 1944 when my father was there. It was restored to its previous appearance after the bombings. Today Mortain is best known for its beautiful landscape, dairy farms, Camembert cheese, and the overwhelming gratitude its citizens still feel for the Americans who liberated them.

The order to seize Mortain that had been personally issued by Adolf Hitler on August 4 was quickly acted upon. As the 30th Infantry prepared to relieve the other divisions in and around Mortain, all came together for a debriefing. It quickly became apparent that detailed maps of the surrounding terrain didn't exist. Because the previous battle with the Nazis had been swift and furious, no one had had time to draw up maps. The Americans had secured Mortain with no expectation that it would ever again be the center of armed combat. Unfortunately, not too far away, German commander Von Kluge had just given the order for his 400 Panzers to start moving toward Mortain.

On the morning of August 6, it was sunny and beautiful in Mortain. At 2:30 in the afternoon, the first sign of the enemy appeared. It was a lone plane carefully scouting the landscape and noting the American positions. Battle-seasoned infantryman on the ground, without even looking up, could now instantly identify a German plane from the distinct sound of its engine. Immediately the order was given for my dad's infantry to improve their positions and dig in. Based on maps from that time obtained from several still-living Mortain historians, Dad's actual location was in a thick forest slightly south of the city just below Hill 314.

As the company started digging in, the soldiers discovered they could only dig down eight inches or so before hitting large rocks. Their commanders told them to do whatever was needed to increase the depth of their foxholes. In some instances grenades were used to break up the terrain. Finally Company H was secure and ready for the impending battle. Once again, the enemy was scouting the area. High in the sky a group of five German planes approached and then flew off. Everyone on the ground knew this was only the start of bigger things to come.

Chow lines were being set up as the planes left the area. Company H was about to have a hearty hot meal with all the fixings. Dad ate his fill. My father would not have another hot meal for ten months.

The soldiers had two days' worth of K-rations. It was evident to everyone that hot meals weren't going to be served again anytime soon. Army intelligence reported that the Germans were closing in on Mortain from the east and the south. It would not be long before they were in the vicinity of the town. Every commander's portable radio was broadcasting the following message: Hill 314 must be held at all costs. The Germans need Hill 314 and will do anything to get it. Failure is not an option.

By 8 p.m. everyone was fed, fully dug in, and waiting. Some of the troops quietly visited with each other as they finished their preparations. My dad's location was deep in the forest, and a veil of darkness started to creep over him. He moved his jeep into a secure area away from any open roads. He and three others were ordered to secure extra water from a working well located at a small French farmhouse called *La Fieffe de l'Ermitage* about two and a half miles from Company H's position.

FINDING THE RELIC
AND CAPTURE BY THE GERMANS

The entire area was under American control and deemed safe. It had not been possible to drive the jeep to the farmhouse because of a very rugged hillside. As Dad and his men left their base camp and started to walk to the well, they encountered thick forests and steep hills. Arriving at the top of a hill, the men found themselves directly next to *Chapelle Saint-Michel*, which had been built by French monks in the thirteenth century. The chapel had sustained damage during the battle between the Americans and Germans several weeks earlier.

Arriving at the chapel, my father entered and said a quick prayer for himself and all the soldiers of the 30th Division. Sadness once again filled his heart as he reviewed the events of the last eight weeks. It had been quite a journey so far. He was just glad to be alive and have his chance to say a prayer. Slightly on edge as the darkness settled in, he looked down at the rubble and spied a small relic among the ruins of the church. His army training had taught him to ignore such things because they might be booby-trapped.

Starting to walk away, he decided he wanted this relic as a reminder of his belief in God. He also thought it might protect him from the enemy. He bent down, looking for signs of wire or explosives. Deciding to take a chance, he closed his eyes and carefully wrapped his fingers around the oval-shaped relic, gently lifting it out of the pile of debris.

His heart was beating so fast he thought he might pass out from fear, but nothing exploded. He opened his eyes and saw in his hand a glass dome with a hand-carved stone image of the Blessed Mother holding the Christ Child. He was amazed by the detailed carving in the stone. It had the look and feel of having been made by someone with a lot of patience a very long time ago. Dad was amazed that the glass dome had not broken when it fell to the floor of the chapel. He put the relic in his inside pocket and left the church.

The soldiers arrived at the well enveloped in a false sense of security. The area was extremely quiet, and instinctively my dad wondered if something might not be right. Wanting to avoid seeming overly paranoid, he and the others collected the water and checked their guns to make sure they were ready to fire. Since intelligence reports had not indicated any need for immediate concern, Dad's group discounted their paranoia and continued on. Gaining confidence, my father started looking around to make sure that all was secure. As he moved in to fill his canteens, he realized his two companions had disappeared into the darkness. His heart started to race. Not sure what to do, he softly called out their names in the darkness. Perhaps they'd wandered off out of his hearing. To his relief, he found them behind the barn relieving themselves. They started to nervously joke about losing contact with one another. My dad told them he'd been a little upset at being left alone at the well. What if they'd been victims of an ambush? The men collected their things, picked up their guns, and set out through the forest to return to Company H.

Light clouds were overhead on a moonless night, but it wasn't all that dark. Making their way past the well into a field surrounded by medium-sized hedgerows, the men cautiously and quietly found their way back to camp. A slight chill went through my dad's body as his pant legs absorbed the dew off the long grass. Approaching a set of trees that led into a small forest, they negotiated a path around cows grazing in the field. Once again, my dad's sixth sense kicked in. Something didn't seem right. But cautiously they continued on. One of the men quietly mentioned that this entire area seemed free of Germans. "You just never know," my dad responded, suggesting they quicken their pace.

He wondered how anyone could possibly hear any other sounds over the deafening roar of crickets and other insects. If the enemy were close by, he thought, they certainly wouldn't be able to hear them. Cautiously they entered the small forest looming before them and soon had made it back to Company H camp in one piece.

Immediately they learned that their commander had orders to move all four jeeps and some of the supplies away from the area. They were told to drive them north along the edge of the forest in the general direction of La Fieffe de l'Ermitage. It went through my dad's mind that it was just like the army to do everything twice. The trip back to where they had just been was going to take longer, because they had to drive around the large hill and follow several roads. Remembering how scary it had been before, Dad knew he would feel more secure inside the jeep.

With the jeeps packed and ready, the order was given to move out at about 9:45. Slowly making their way in the darkness, the only sound the eight men in the four jeeps could hear was the rumbling of their engines. No one talked much while navigating the rough terrain in the dark woods. The lights on the jeeps' exteriors were shielded with blinders to limit the amount of light being emitted. Dad's jeep was fourth in line, in the graveyard position. Soon they were west of the farm they'd visited only hours before, driving through the dark, secluded countryside.

Moving slowly on a makeshift road through the forest, it was difficult to see ten feet ahead. The convoy entered a thick line of trees along the road when suddenly an enormous explosion occurred in the front of it. A blinding fireball instantly engulfed the first jeep. My dad recalled what happened after that:

> I'm driving along in my jeep, when the number one jeep up front of me hit a land mine. I'm the fourth and last jeep in line. I see the number one go up. I don't know whether I'm the next man or not. There is debris flying everywhere and now bullets from an undisclosed location.

The two men in the front jeep did not survive the explosion, but despite the gunfire, no one else was hit. Quickly taking out his gun and preparing for battle, Dad realized he had no idea where to aim or shoot in the dense forest surrounding the convoy. He aimlessly fired off several rounds from his pistol. Within seconds the American soldiers heard behind them a loud, distinct German voice above the commotion, yelling "Halt, halt!" along with other commands in English: "You are now prisoners of the German Army. Lay down your guns and immediately get out of the vehicle. Surrender. Surrender."

Out of the dark eight German soldiers emerged. How could this happen? my shocked dad wondered. The Germans had not been anywhere around this area, or had they? His mind racing, Dad's first thought was how to radio his commanders to alert them to the presence of German soldiers near Hill 314. His second thought, as he remembered it, was how mad he was at himself for not paying closer attention to his earlier instincts and paranoia. Stupid! he thought. Somehow the Germans had pulled a counterattack, arriving back in the area unnoticed. Harsh and stern, the Germans clearly meant business. The six Americans were not allowed to talk and were instructed to hold their wrists and extend their arms high over their heads. Any variation from these orders would result in being shot on the spot.

The eight Germans appeared to be of the SS variety. Two spoke perfect English; the others spoke only German. The Americans were searched and their guns, bullets, grenades, and water taken from them. Even their K-rations were confiscated, along with their helmets. But the Germans didn't find my mother's picture taped to the edge of my dad's undershirt. Even more amazing, the German who searched my dad found the relic, looked at it, gazed into my father's eyes for a moment—creating some unspeakable connection between them—and handed it back, telling him to return it to his pocket. How odd, thought my father. Why did he do this? he wondered. Was it because he had a flicker of compassion for me? He locked the guard's actions away in his memory.

After the men were searched, things went from bad to worse. Suddenly my father's heart was racing again. He didn't speak German, and now all the orders were being barked in German. It was as if someone had turned on a faucet of hate. One of the Germans extended his rifle butt into my dad's chest, ordering him to "move out." My dad was now in extreme pain and wondering if his ribs had been broken. He could barely catch his breath and it hurt to walk, but he proceeded onward. The two American soldiers nearest my dad suffered the same treatment, except one of them was jabbed and cut with a bayonet.

The six Americans, now petrified with fear, were unable to openly communicate with one other. As they walked in total silence, my dad's mind was going a mile a minute. What was going to happen to him? Where were they being taken to? Would he survive this ordeal? Strangely, none of the Germans had taken the time to interrogate them, and this seemed odd to my dad. He remembered how brief his training had been about what to do if captured. "Tell them nothing except your name, rank and serial number," he'd been told. Dad silently repeated this to himself over and over again as they walked for miles in the darkness over the fields of Mortain.

My dad began to worry that he would be tortured when he refused to give the Nazis any information beyond his name, rank, and serial number. What if they didn't give a damn about obeying the Geneva Conventions, the rules about how to treat prisoners of war? From experience, my dad knew that the SS variety of Nazis did not give a hoot about right or wrong. What the SS wanted, they got—and they got it fast. It didn't matter if human lives stood in the way, for the Third Reich represented Hitler's finest—a ruthless killing machine that stopped for no one. Dad had learned this definitively weeks before when he helped bury the French family of six near St. LO. His memories of that sad morning only made him more fearful.

Several hours had passed since his capture. Arriving at a small wooded area, the SS guards met up with others of the same ilk. This new group

The Nodurft Twins

Tim and Jim Nodurft were identical twins and the same age as my father. Born in 1922, the three of them grew up together in West Virginia. By age seven, they'd become inseparable. Dad was drafted a month earlier than Tim and Jim, but somehow they all ended up in the 30th Infantry. Shortly before the start of Operation Cobra, Dad visited with his two pals. Many years after the war he gave testimony to a Veterans Administration doctor about his war experiences. In the transcript my dad talked about the last time he saw the Nodurft twins:

> I saw these two boys just prior to the bombing. I talked to Tim and Jim and we shared a laugh together, remembering the good times we'd had. The time was getting real close for the start of Operation Cobra, so we needed to take our battle positions. After they blew the hell out of us and the town, I went back to see how Tim and Jim had fared, and I talked to a kid that was in the foxhole adjacent to theirs and he said they both got killed.

> Well, that has left a mark on my mind ever since then. [The transcript indicates that Dad had started to cry.] I came home after discharge, I was married, and then I went down to my mother and father's house—they still lived in the home that I was inducted into the army from. I went to see the memorial of the boys that I knew from that area who'd been inducted with me, and there at the bottom were Tim and Jim's names with gold stars. So I'm standing there, just like right now, I can't help it . . . [Dad was now sobbing]. Tim's real name was Claude H. Nodurft and Jim's real name was Francis R. Nodurft.

of Nazis had also captured American troops. Gunfire had erupted, with the Americans unfortunately suffering the losses. The Americans were assembled into one large group by the SS guards; my dad realized he had seen most of the eight other soldiers before. The SS guards informed all the prisoners in perfect English that no one was to talk. My dad's eyes searched through the darkness as he tried to recognize the individual faces of his buddies. He saw that three were injured, one severely; four others lay dead. One, a PFC, had escaped injury and was ordered to join my dad's circle. This was more sadness and horror for my father to take in. The darkness of the night only seemed to make the situation worse.

Now the SS guards were speaking and shouting in German and talking heatedly among themselves. One of them hastily pulled out a pistol, turned, walked over to the three injured soldiers lying on the ground, and systematically shot them all dead. The sound of the gunfire echoed in the woods and quickly faded.

My father almost lost it. But he restrained himself because he knew that if he reacted to the shootings, he would be placing the life of every American soldier in his circle in jeopardy. He told my mother after the war that he had worried about the other men in his group behaving foolishly, but no one did. Despite feeling emotionally overwhelmed, my dad that night had somehow managed to retain his composure.

———

Killing the severely injured soldiers rather than leaving them behind served two purposes for the Germans. First, dead American soldiers could not provide their squad leaders with valuable information on the positions and movements of the Nazis. Second, leaving behind the dead soldiers allowed the Germans to advance more quickly. During wartime the ethics surrounding the deaths of soldiers can become very blurry. Unspeakable and inhuman atrocities often occur. The Nazis of the SS variety were so skilled at killing that when war crimes were later uncovered and investigated, it often seemed that the victims had been killed in heated battle.

One of the SS guards, who didn't speak English, began to booby-trap the body of one of the slain soldiers. My dad and his fellow POWs became extremely angry and upset. Observing this reaction, the remaining SS guards forcibly moved the entire group away from the scene and started shouting in German in an effort to distract them. From that moment on Dad could no longer control his hatred of the Nazis. He detested them and what they were doing to the rest of Europe. Dad actually thought for a moment about trying to gain control of this terrible situation. Quickly coming to his senses, he realized his efforts would be in vain because the Americans were outnumbered three to one. Somehow the soldiers all remained calm, evading the cruel fate of their slain buddies.

The German guards once again gave the order to move out. This time a gentler rifle butt was thrust into the chests of some of the men. My dad noticed the subtle change, speculating that perhaps this guard had a chink in his armor and was feeling some regret over the brutal killings. Dad assessed the German soldiers, deciding that four were strong leaders and ruthless killers and the rest mere pawns in a horrible chess game. My dad made a mental note of this and later in his life as a POW used this type of observation to his advantage.

The POWs once again were under way, this time accompanied by additional SS guards. Any sense of time had vanished for my dad. His only possessions were his summer uniform, his dog tags (with his army P-38 can opener attached), my mother's picture, and the relic. As he plodded through the dark and muddy fields, he wondered how long it would take for his parents and Eleanore to learn that he had been taken prisoner. What would they think? he wondered.

The captured soldiers marched through the night away from Mortain. The need to sleep was becoming a nagging and persistent problem for each of the men. The initial rush of fear had passed, to be replaced by an overwhelming need for sleep. Thirst and hunger were also increasing with every step. The Nazis began to drink my dad's water, and they snacked on the Americans' bread and cheese as they walked. No food or drink was offered to the American POWs. Far off in the distance, the low rumble of German Panzers could be heard above the quietness of the night. The Panzers were certainly rolling into the town of Mortain. The sound of gunfire was increasing in intensity, but still seemed far off in the distance. Not once did any of the SS guards ever mention or acknowledge the sounds of the nearby war. They just kept marching on.

It started to drizzle, and soon a soft rain began to fall. It was the middle of the night; the guards finally instructed them to lie down in the rain and go to sleep. How do you sleep, my dad wondered, when you are soaked to the bones and cold? They found a small patch of trees and bedded down in the tall, wet grass. The SS guards took out their rain gear and, leaning up against another group of trees, prepared to stand watch over their captors. With every breath my dad felt the pain in his ribs, a sad reminder of what he had endured only hours before. His final thoughts before falling asleep centered on the three men who had just been executed. He prayed for them and their families before drifting off to sleep.

NAZI DEPRAVITY

"*A ufstehen, Aufstehen,*" an SS guard announced with a swift kick to my dad's legs. Jarred but not really awake, Dad for a moment forgot about the situation he was in. His eyes finally opened, and reality hit him with full force. He sprang quickly to his feet. Dawn was visible in the sky, and Dad was able to see the faces of his German captors more clearly. Strangely, if the uniforms had been removed, he realized, they would have looked like any other man he might have met in any small town in Europe. He began to wonder about each man's personal life. Were they married? Did any of them have children? Did they have a mother and father still living? Were their parents proud of them? Dad was unable to imagine how any parent could be proud of these men.

Questions continued to plague his young mind. How did these men end up believing in the Hitler machine? But most of all, he wondered how they could have stood silently by while their comrade executed three American soldiers in cold blood.

Soon a Nazi guard shouted, *"Bewegung!"* Then the voice of another German guard spoke in English: "Move, move . . ." They started walking again. Far off in the distance they could hear the action brewing in the French countryside. Mortain was now the focus of the Germans, and the intensity of the battle was increasing. Thirsty, hungry, and craving coffee, my father marched onward. After a short while, they arrived back in the area where they had originally been captured. The Americans were now puzzled and confused. Dad estimated they had walked ten miles since their capture and were now back where they had started out the night before.

The Germans began to push the prisoners, forcing them into a straight line facing the commander. Speaking calmly and in near-perfect English, a guard asked each of them what they did in the U.S. Army. Dad was first in line: "I drive a jeep," he said, and then stopped talking. Walking toward him, the commander pressed his face close to my father's and said, "You come with me."

My father, shaking in fear, followed the Nazi. Back in line, the other Americans were asked the same question by other English-speaking guards. The commander leading the way, my father was followed by another guard with his gun aimed directly at him to make sure he didn't try to escape. They walked through the trees and arrived at some American jeeps parked in the middle of some very tall bushes. Pointing at the closest jeep, the commander told my father to "get in."

Dad did not have the time to figure out what company this jeep had belonged to; he jumped in and awaited further orders. Soon the other prisoners were making their way out of the forest to the area near my father. The Germans instructed the Americans to take the other two jeeps, and two of my dad's buddies jumped in the front drivers' seats and waited. Next, most of the guards climbed in, taking all the remaining seats. The other guards surrounded the jeeps and ordered the Americans to drive into the woods, away from Mortain. Every German gun was pointed at the prisoners to ensure that they wouldn't drive off in the wrong direction. My dad thought, Where the hell could I go, if I wanted to?

The jeeps made their way through the forest in rugged terrain for about three hours. They were definitely driving away from Mortain. Now the sounds of battle were far off in the distance. My father's heart was filled with anxiety, because he knew his remaining company was now experiencing full combat battle. When they'd discovered in the morning roll call that he wasn't there, he knew his name would have been placed in that day's morning report as "missing in battle." Thinking about this made him even more upset. "Missing" meant the army had no idea at all where you were. Either you'd been killed but not yet found, you'd been vaporized by a bomb and would never be found, or you'd been captured by the enemy. A cold shiver ran down my dad's spine as he assessed his situation. He was now a German prisoner of war, and it could take weeks before someone figured it out.

———————

Arriving at their destination, everyone quickly realized that a battle had recently taken place. The American prisoners were told to get out of the jeeps and line up. No English was spoken, only German, but the Americans were beginning to understand what the commands meant. Everyone sprang into action. Approximately fifty SS guards were alive and suffering from post-battle shock. Even more dead and wounded were lying about everywhere. It was a horrific scene, with body parts, blood, and guts strewn across the ground. One of the Americans vomited. My father somehow kept it together, blocking the carnage out of his mind. The commander spoke in English, telling them to "get to work."

A commander who had survived the attack instructed some of the Americans to start digging a large hole at the bottom of an existing crater that had been created by an artillery shell. Thank God, my dad thought, because the size of the hole they would need to bury all these Germans was going to have to be huge. Dad started digging the mass grave with the other prisoners. His chest hurt a little but he was able to continue digging. He was relieved that he didn't have any broken ribs. The wounded were being cared for and moved from the scene by the SS guards; no Americans were allowed to touch them. My father and others carefully lifted the dead bodies and body parts from the battleground and placed them in the freshly dug hole. By the time they had finished burying the German dead in the mass grave, the Americans were covered in dirt and blood.

The guards now instructed my father and the others to take large cans of oil and pour them over the piled bodies. In his journal my father wrote that the oil looked like tar. When the oil had been spread around, one of the German commanders walked over to the mass grave, paused for a moment, shook his head in disgust, and said, *"Idioten,"* which in English means "Idiots." He put a cigarette in his mouth and took a match from his pocket. Carefully lighting his cigarette, he took a quick puff. He looked up at the sky before tossing the lit match into the grave, along with his glowing cigarette. In an instant the oil ignited, quickly spreading flames across the grave. The fumes from the oil that had landed far down in the hole made the flames ripple like a blanket of fire. Horrified, my father was even more convinced now that these were real bad guys. It seemed to him that the commander was pissed off at the dead for having the temerity to be killed in battle. Or maybe he was just one very bad SS commander and didn't care about anything but himself, his pride, and Hitler. This really concerned my father, for he and the others were in the custody of this commander, and so far they hadn't been treated very well. As he watched the mass grave evolving into an inferno, my father prayed for the dead.

━━━━━━━━━

As thick black smoke rose into the sky, the guards ordered everyone to move out of the area quickly. The rising smoke would be a dead giveaway to the Allied forces. The German wounded who couldn't walk were taking up all the jeep seats. The other wounded Germans were told to walk alongside the jeeps. But the severely wounded Germans were abandoned on the ground without any medical attention—their commanders were leaving them behind.

As the Americans watched, the Germans began barking commands at each other. Many of the German soldiers were not happy about the fate of their badly wounded comrades. Several of the men on the ground cried out, realizing they were being left to die. Strangely, no medic was anywhere in sight. My dad was ordered to climb into his jeep and be ready to move.

Dad scanned the inside of the jeep while he awaited his orders. He noticed candy wrappers similar to the ones he'd discarded several days before. Further scrutiny confirmed that he was in the same jeep he'd been driving when he was captured. My dad knew this jeep very well— he'd packed it himself with provisions. He glanced down at his hands, noticing how dirty and blood-stained they were. His clothes were also a filthy mess. Hunger and intense thirst plagued him. It was now more than thirteen hours since his capture, and he still hadn't been offered any food or drink. He started to develop a slight headache from dehydration. Finally the Germans issued the order to drive.

One of Dad's buddies quietly mentioned that he knew they were moving away from the lines of battle and heading for the interior of France, away from the war. They didn't know it yet, but ultimately they were going to end up somewhere in Germany far from any type of battle. It would be a safe haven for the Germans and a nightmare for the American prisoners of war. Onward they went.

No one was allowed to talk. The Americans squirmed with thirst and hunger. They were becoming so dehydrated that they no longer needed to stop to relieve themselves. My father politely asked his guard if they could have a drink of water, and the response was an absolute "Nein."

It was mid-evening when they arrived at what my dad called CP in his war journal. This was a large command post full of Nazi soldiers. One of the commanders now instructed his men to give their prisoners as much water as they could drink. More than sixteen hours had passed without food or water for the Americans. My dad told my mother that he never saw a group of men drink so much water. Having had their fill of water, the Americans' bellies sloshed audibly as they walked to the interior of the Command Post. Some of the German guards laughed out loud at them. My dad knew that the laughs masked a killing machine ready to explode at a moment's notice.

The SS guards' tactic for mobilizing American prisoners was to push them around with rifles, guns, or batons. Treating the prisoners in this way ensured that the SS could dominate, intimidate, and control them. The SS loudly barked orders in German, speaking harshly in short sentences. The guards would also go up to the faces of the Americans and stare directly into their eyes when interrogating them. The SS used the German language as a weapon, especially against those who didn't understand it. Most of the soldiers captured with my father didn't understand German.

My father was a very confident person, except during his time in the army. The war and its atrocities slowly wore away his confidence. By the time he entered prison camp, his emotions were raw.

Once the POWs had conquered their thirst, the SS used their batons to push Dad and the other Americans into a single line. Dad was very scared again. He anxiously awaited his turn as the Americans were taken one at a time into the tent of the commander. After each soldier was done being interrogated, the guards ushered him out the back of the tent so he couldn't see or gesture to the American coming in next. Finally my dad was pushed inside the tent for questioning. As he entered, the canvas door was closed behind him. An excerpt from my father's war diary about that experience:

When I entered the tent, they started asking me a lot of things at once. Of course I did not say a thing. That made them mad as hell. In the background, there was a German lieutenant that understood English very well. He started talking to me.

He asked what I did, and I told him once again I drove a jeep. I decided to ask him directly if I could get some things out of the jeep. He asked me if one of the jeeps were mine. I replied, "Yes." Slightly amazed at my line of questioning, he put a guard with me, and I was told to go to the jeep and get what I wanted. I thought maybe they had cleared out the contents of the jeep by now but this was not the case. Everything was there just like I left it. Even the cigarettes were there!

With the SS guard pointing his rifle at him, my father inventoried the contents of the jeep:

(35)	Cartons of American Cigarettes
(2)	Cases of K-Rations
(3)	Cases of C-Rations
(1)	Case of D-Rations

Collecting it all, he and the Germans brought it back inside the tent.

The German lieutenant then asked me if all the cigarettes were mine. I replied, "Yes." He then said for me to take all that I could carry with me. Pausing for a moment, he also told me to take one can of rations from each box. I was sure glad I did this later.

My father ended up with six cans of rations and some restored confidence. He'd hit the jackpot and was very happy. But he wondered why the lieutenant had given him the supplies. Learning from this experience, he promised himself that in the future he would listen carefully, evaluate thoughtfully, and be as forthcoming as he could with each SS guard. He had a hunch that these tactics would make his time as a POW more tolerable. He also vowed to himself to never compromise the army or the United States' position in Europe. From now on, my father would be looking for opportunities to benefit himself personally while in the custody of the German Army. He understood that he was walking a very fine line, and that his plans could backfire on him at any moment. Despite the risk, he decided it was worth it in order to survive.

My dad's decision to ask the lieutenant if he could get some supplies out of the jeep helped save his life later on. When the lieutenant was finished with my dad, he was pushed out the back of the tent with his pockets full of supplies. Standing with his guard, he immediately opened a can of rations and quickly ate them. The meager amount of food did not take away the burning hunger pangs but his existence became more comfortable, at least for a while. An excerpt from his diary:

After they interrogated the hell out of us, the SS guards could still not get any information they wanted. This made us all really happy.

When we all came back together from our interrogations we were all amazed that everyone received several cans of rations and some cigarettes. Silently I kept my mouth shut for I had more cigarettes, rations than anybody. Thank God my uniform was larger than it needed to be because I was hoping no one would notice my pockets bulging with the extra items they gave me. I now knew I could charm the commanders and use it to my advantage.

Quickly the German guards rousted all the Americans, placing them in a nearby field and making them dig holes. The ground was hard and rocky and the shovels worn—the handles kept breaking. The perimeter of the field was ringed with armed guards who would immediately shoot to kill if any of the men tried to run off. A few minutes later, an American P47 circled high overhead. Dad and his buddy became very frightened, remembering the horrors of Operation Cobra. It didn't seem plausible to hope that the P47 would be able to distinguish Americans from Germans from the air. Suddenly, the plane turned sharply and headed toward another field.

As it swooped down closer to the field, suddenly the P47 started bombing the hell out of this field. It was loaded with Germans. As quick as it came, it then left. Immediately the German guards who were watching us came in and told us we were moving out.

It was late afternoon of the second day of their ordeal. Dad and the other prisoners were quickly assembled in a single line and headed off into the forest for cover. Several other Americans who had also been captured earlier had joined my dad's group, which now consisted of twelve American prisoners being guarded by twenty-four SS guards. The SS guards were going to make damn sure that nobody escaped.

It was my good luck, sixty-four years later, to meet one of the Americans who'd been imprisoned with my dad. Mark Copenhaver was also a member of the 30th Division, and he'd been captured separately around the same time as my father. Mark graciously told me his story in March

2008, and it aligns perfectly with what my father wrote in his journal. Mark vaguely remembers my father, but due to the ravages of time and dementia his memory is not what it once was. However, this eighty-five-year-old veteran does remember exactly what it was like to be an American prisoner of war in World War II:

> No matter what happens to my mind, the feelings from this experience will never go away. It will always be there for as long as I live. The experience is forever emblazoned in my mind, no matter how many details I may forget. It was the saddest and most terrible time of my life.

THE FIFTY-FOUR-DAY MARCH
TO GERMANY BEGINS

It was now late evening, and the SS guards continued pushing the American prisoners to keep a strict pace as they walked. They started at 5 p.m. and marched well into the early morning of the next day. The Americans had no extra food with them, except for the rations each man had been given earlier. My dad waited as long as he could before opening up the only D-ration he had, because he knew it was designed for survival and contained the most calories. D-Rations were three four-ounce bars of chocolate that tasted like a boiled potato. He quickly ate it to avoid the notice of the guards, and it gave him the strength to continue walking. The Germans were not going to let up. By 3 a.m. many miles had been covered, and all the men were exhausted. Finding a barn, the guards allowed them to sleep nestled in some clean hay. The relief of sleep only lasted for three hours.

Waking to another day, the American prisoners remained exhausted and starving. The Germans, who enjoyed their fill of rations, never suffered from an energy problem. Unfortunately, they were becoming more hostile and insulting, physically jabbing any Americans who were unable to keep up the necessary pace. Finally, one of the SS Guards realized that lack of food was causing the problems with the Americans, and they stopped in the next French town to find some food.

The Germans believed they were entitled to take anything they wanted. Several of the guards stormed a bakery that had just opened and demanded bread for the twelve American prisoners. It was early, and most of that day's bread was still in the oven. But the baker was full of understanding and compassion for the Americans and quickly rustled up any food he could find to give to them.

The gracious baker also offered wine and loaded a large basket to overflowing, with more bread than anyone could possibly eat over several days, and gave it to the guards. They grabbed the basket out of the arms of the baker, pushed him aside, and started sorting the larger loaves from the smaller ones. The guards took the wine and filled their packs with most of the bread, leaving the remaining loaves in the basket for the Americans to carry.

My father's tells about this incident in his journal: "After all the confusion, we each received a piece of bread from the Nazis that measured 3" long by 1" wide by ½" thick. That was all of it. Basically it was a bread stick."

The French hated the Nazis and loved the Americans. The French baker wished that roles had been reversed and the Americans had captured the Nazis. My father could tell by the look in the baker's eyes that, given the chance, he would have shot the guards dead in an instant.

The Americans were allowed to drink their fill of water as they left the town. But after being under way again for several hours, my dad was starving. He had four cans of rations left, and his head was exploding in pain. He calculated that they had most likely walked thirty or more miles the day before, and today their journey would be even longer. My dad had to decide whether to eat two cans of rations now to give him the strength to continue walking and to stop his headache, or stretch out the rations over the next several days.

Agonizing about this, Dad continued on for some time. Finally he decided that he'd be better off eating the two cans of rations now. He needed to ask permission of the guards. He thought about the promise he'd made to himself to listen, observe, and use kindness to get what he needed in spite of always being pissed off at the guards. Dad observed that the attitudes of some of the other soldiers in his group were on a par with those of the guards. "Why me?" or "Poor me" radiated from their bodies. My dad knew that these guys were never going to be able to gain the upper hand because they were consumed by hatred and resentment over what was happening to them. Dad understood it was essential to never give the guards any back-talk. Kindness was going to be key to his survival.

Dad had figured out that one guard in the group was clearly different from the others. He was kind and gentle, with more compassion than the others. Building a relationship with him was going to be essential. Most of the guards considered the Americans a liability and a real pain in the ass.

Feeling unsure about how the kind guard might react, Dad proceeded with his plan. The guard understood some English. Dad approached him, gesturing that he wanted to eat the two cans of rations and holding out the three cigarettes with his other hand. The guard glanced down at the cigarettes and smiled slightly. He knew exactly what my father wanted and immediately grabbed the cigarettes from his hand, saying in German, *"Grünes licht"* or "Go ahead."

The hundreds of cigarettes in his possession had become an important part of his survival. American cigarettes were often better than money during the war. He would limit his smoking and use the cigarettes to his advantage. When nicotine addiction was driving a Nazi guard crazy, trading cigarettes for food or favors became the norm between enemies. Most soldiers stockpiled them.

Staying right next to the guard, my dad opened the rations with his P-38 can opener and ate them. This was a test to see if any of the other guards had a problem with what had just happened. To Dad's surprise, nobody seemed to care. He had now learned a valuable survival lesson. Building relationships and handing out cigarettes would work very much in his favor over the next months. Soon his headache was going away, and his confidence was growing. Unfortunately this was only one small win for him. Over the next ten months difficult circumstances would repeatedly challenge him.

After what felt to the Americans like 100 miles of walking, the SS decided to stop at 11 p.m. and bed down in an abandoned house. As usual, Dad and the others were starving. This time one of the guards announced in English that they could eat the rations they had with them. They all decided to eat their fill to be ready for the next day's march. Quietly the men made a plan between them to keep an eye out the next day for berries, vegetables, and bugs—anything edible. Dad eagerly consumed his last two cans of rations; with a full belly and in a state of exhaustion, he soon drifted off to sleep.

Dad wrote about the next day in his journal:

The next morning we were woke up very early. The sun was just coming up on the horizon. The guards gave us each a loaf of bread between six men. What I am about to write, you will not believe. Stamped on the side of the bread [was a label saying] it was made in 1935! The outside of the bread was very hard but the inside was still good.

Bread was the staple during the war, if you were lucky to get some. It was entirely possible that the bread my dad was writing about had been made nine years before. Most likely it was found in the rubble of an old house that had suffered a bomb blast.

The head guard informed the American prisoners as they walked that today they didn't have far to go. What the hell do they mean? my father wondered. Every prisoner knew they were being herded like cattle to the interior of Germany, where the Third Reich still reigned and the prison camps were plentiful. My dad guessed, though, that the immediate destination was Paris. One hour turned into three and then into five. You could never trust what the SS guards were telling you—they specialized in deception and lies. The miserable march continued.

Finally they arrived at a clearing between stands of dense woods. Drawing closer, they noticed a group of French men, obviously displaced by the war, living in the clearing and using the woods for their cover. The familiar smell of a charcoal fire filled the humid summer air. Concerned by the approaching Germans, the French cautiously walked toward the SS guards, raising their arms to show they weren't hiding weapons. Smiling and making direct eye contact, the French tried to engage the American prisoners in conversation and offer them food. But the guards moved in immediately, preventing further contact between the French and the Americans.

One of the guards approached a large stove, lifting the lid on a simmering pot. "Soup," he announced. Then turning to one of the French men, he ordered him to give a cup of soup to each prisoner. The man enthusiastically met the guard's request, repeatedly filling four cups and passing them among the prisoners. When a cup of the soup came to my dad, he cherished the homemade flavor as he quickly devoured it. I heard my dad say many times that this was the best-tasting soup he ever ate in his life. Now the Americans were told to walk a short distance into the woods where, for the first time since their capture, they were placed in an open-backed truck and transported to an undisclosed destination.

The men's energy level was so low that boarding the truck was a difficult task. Even worse, fresh cow manure covered the truck bed. There were no seats, and the smell was awful. The Nazis harshly pushed them into the truck. This return of cruel force was probably the result of Dad's group of guards meeting up with other members of the SS. Dad was sure they were showing off.

The truck was soon under way, and, fortunately, the wind lessened the putrid smell and made the ride tolerable. Riding in a truck was better than walking and burning up calories no one had to spare. It was late in the evening, and the Americans as usual had no food or water. When they finally stopped at an old French fort, they were told to get off the truck and go inside.

One of the American prisoners, whom my dad did not know, finally snapped. He began to shout with anger and disgust, making threats against the guards. This was a grave mistake. A guard raised his rifle, pointed it at the prisoner, and fired. The sound of the rifle fire echoed off the walls of the fort. The shot had narrowly missed the prisoner's right ear. He began to beg for mercy, as the others watched in silent horror. The American pleaded one final time for his life, but it was too late. The guard cocked his gun, corrected his aim, pulled the trigger, and placed a bullet right between his eyes. As the prisoner dropped to the floor, the Nazi shouted, "Bastard" and asked the others if they wanted to be next.

No one said a word. Dad was horrified, now fully understanding the wisdom of his resolve to never talk back. Panic and fear, coupled with rage, seized the minds of the remaining eleven Americans as they tried to come to terms with what they had just witnessed. The guard told the men to take the soldier's body and dump it outside of the fort. The men did what they were told, their eyes welling with tears. Recalling this terrible moment with my mother, Dad said he had been exploding inside with anger but somehow had managed to hang on to his composure.

They were the only ones staying in the large and spacious fort. The guards decided to lock all eleven men inside a small windowless room, no larger than 10' x 10'. The only available light came from the candles in the adjacent room glowing through the holes at the bottom of the door. Suddenly the door flew open, and eight green apples were thrown into the room for the men to share. "A very cruel act against us once again," my dad told my mother.

The men bit into the apples, discovering worms inside. Some grabbed the wriggling worms and ate them for nourishment. Soon every morsel of the apples had been eaten except the seeds. Still hungry, the men now struggled with how they were going to sleep in the extremely cramped room. To relieve themselves, the men had to knock on the door to be let outside, where the guards watched over them at gunpoint. The prisoners' most basic private acts were under control of the SS guards, which only depressed the already low morale of the men. Sleeping required them to lie together in impossibly close quarters. With all the body heat and no ventilation, it was extremely uncomfortable. Somehow they drifted off to sleep.

———————

Several hours later the familiar sounds of American P-47 bombers and their bombs began to rock the area around the fort. Jarred awake and panic-stricken, the Americans realized they were under attack by their own forces. The pilots of the P-47s had no idea they were dropping bombs near American POWs. The pilots were looking for Germans and trying to disrupt their movements and camps. The guards immediately left the fort to take cover in the woods, leaving my dad and the others locked in the tiny room. As hard as they tried, they could not break down the door. They protected themselves by putting their arms over their head to block falling debris. The Americans remained silent as the bombs exploded everywhere around them.

Vibrations from the bombs caused fragments of plaster and cement to rain down on the Americans. Dust filled the room, and it became difficult to breathe. Many of the men were coughing. A stray bomb hit the room next to the prisoners, but no one was harmed. Soon the roaring planes left the area, and all was quiet once again.

The Nazi guards rushed back into the fort and quickly opened the door to the small room. Without saying a word, the guards hustled everyone into the larger room. The prisoners' faces, hair, and clothes were covered in white powder. Dad could see through a hole in the massive wall that boxcars on a nearby railroad track were burning fiercely and lighting up the night sky. The Germans were talking among themselves, probably about the bombing attack. My father's last thoughts before falling asleep that night were of Eleanore and how much he missed her and of how happy he was that American pilots had successfully bombed the hell out of the German train, leaving it in complete destruction.

Morning came quickly, and soon the quiet was once again marred by P-38s high overhead. This time the Germans rousted everyone out of the fort and into the cover of the woods. My dad saw the five bombers swoop down over the smoldering boxcars on a fly-by. An excerpt from his journal:

> I was happy to see the American bombers but they had no idea we American POWs were anywhere near this area. Obviously they came over last night's targets to see how well they did. From what I could tell they bombed the hell out the railroad cars, because it was a total loss.

> So close, yet so far—we would all imagine we were being rescued, and the bombers were able to gun down every last Nazi guard, releasing us from our misery. Instead they just dropped their bombs and left.

> Around ten in the morning, several of the guards asked us who knew anything about cooking. We all raised our hands and responded, "We do!" It was sure funny because, no matter what, we were all experts at cooking. Our hunger would now allow us to be perfect chefs. All we wanted was a chance at it. They led us all down to the basement where there was a large stone fireplace for cooking. The guards uncovered a table and on it were rotten vegetables and some potatoes. Speaking German, one said, "Angefangen warden" or "Get started."

> We began to make soup, using pieces of the cement from the fort to cut away the vegetables' rotten areas. No knives were going to be allowed. The guards supplied the water and lit a fire for us. At all times their guns were aimed at us. A very short French man was brought in to the fort. He never said a word, looking us all over and counting the number of Americans and Germans.

> About an hour later he returned, bringing us cake and honey. We were amazed that the guards let this happen. We ate all the soup and the cake drizzled with honey. This French man knew how to make a cake. Unfortunately, it was not possible to get our fill. We were still hungry.

The next morning the Americans awoke to commotion and confusion among the guards. Dad understood that the previous day's meal hadn't been a nice gesture on the part of the guards. Everything was always about them. They were just as tired of bread and food scraps, even if they could have their fill. You could never trust what was going on in the mind of an SS guard. Now it was time to board a truck again and proceed toward Paris. Fearing for their own safety, the guards placed white flags—the universal signal that POWs were present—on the trucks to keep the P-38s and P-47s from bombing them on the highway.

As they traveled down the road to Paris, American planes constantly swooped down for a closer look, tipping their wings to indicate they understood the situation before flying off. Sadly, nothing more could be done for the American POWs. The Allies were a long way off, fighting along the MLR. At this time, it was not going to be possible for anyone to rescue the POWs from the Germans. Allies were being captured every day in France. Once you were a POW, you stayed one until someone could rescue you. It was a pretty hopeless situation.

Later that day tragedy struck along the road. A convoy of German trucks heading to the interior of Germany was transporting many American POWs, and all were killed by American bombs. None of these trucks had white flags attached to them. When my dad's group arrived on the scene, they were horrified to see what had happened. The German guards inspected the carnage, obviously very concerned about the unfolding tragedy. It was clear that several of the guards knew some of the dead Germans inside the trucks.

My father intuitively understood that the guards would soon begin to take out their anger and frustration on him and his fellow prisoners. Sure enough, the guards' treatment of their prisoners changed in a heartbeat. Surveying the carnage before them, the Germans were now really pissed at the Americans. The guards found more white cloth and placed it everywhere they could on the trucks to make it extremely clear that American POWs were aboard.

My father told my mother another horrible story on a night when he was struggling with his past. Dad and the other POWs were able to figure out from the heated discussions they overheard that the senior guards were thinking of grouping all the Americans into one truck and leaving it unmarked as a German vehicle. The plan was to sacrifice two junior guards—one to drive the truck, the other to watch over the POWs. This truck was going to be sent far ahead of the main convoy. The trucks carrying the senior SS guards would be clearly marked as POW trucks. When the American planes approached, they would certainly notice a lone German vehicle with no POW markings and bomb the hell out of it.

Once this death plot was discovered by the POWs, it triggered a wave of terrible fear and rage among the Americans. The POW group stayed very quiet as they strained to overhear what was going to come of this terrible plan. Finally they heard the guard Dad had given the cigarettes to days earlier speak up in German. This guard was not in agreement with the rest of his comrades, objecting to the plan. Dad had been right about his compassion and understanding, guessing that the man had been unwillingly forced into becoming an SS guard. He was straddling a fine line between right and wrong. Somehow he needed to convince the other guards this plan would not work. He also couldn't take the position of the Americans, because he would have been shot. He was in a very tough situation.

After several hours of intense discussion, the Germans finally decided that the plan could not work. The Americans figured out that if the SS guards arrived in Germany without prisoners, they would be labeled AWOL and shot. Every German soldier was needed now more than ever on the front lines to push back against the Allies' increasingly successful invasion of France. It was now clear to the Americans that their SS guards would do whatever it took to remain clear of the front lines of battle. Guarding POWs was their golden opportunity to stay alive.

For the first time in the war, my father began to believe he had a grasp on the mind of a Nazi soldier. Some of these Nazis, he realized, did not want to be fighting this war and had only been drafted into doing so. Some of his captors were human. If you were in the right situation, you could figure it out. The puzzle for my father was to figure out which of the Nazi soldiers were imbued with compassion and understanding and how he, over time, could erode the barriers between them. This was the key to making his life as a POW a little easier. But my father also needed to be equally vigilant in figuring out how to identify which of his captors were ruthless killers. As he reviewed the day's events, he concluded he had been spot-on in his assessments. He now had more confidence and knowledge and understood how to behave with individual guards. Honey gets more than vinegar, he decided, especially with Nazi SS guards.

Coming closer to Paris, the convoy entered Chartres. In his later life, my father did not have fond memories of this town because of a stupid stunt pulled by a senior SS guard. Everyone had exited the trucks and was milling around in a part of the town that had already been destroyed. Suddenly a lone P-38 swooped in for a closer look at the group. The senior guard, standing apart from everyone else, apparently decided he'd had enough of the American planes. He grabbed his rifle and started shooting at the American plane, hitting it in the fuselage. Realizing he'd been hit, the P-38 pilot turned sharply and headed off away from the town. In his excitement, the German turned toward the group, yelling in English, "I got him."

In a matter of seconds, the same plane returned, this time with four more P-38s ready for battle. As they approached, the squadron went into the death dive. Before anyone could move, the plane crews pumped hundreds of bullets into the SS guard who'd taken the shot at the P-38. After finishing him off, they approached the rest of the group. My dad and the other POWs were already on the run. The guards were following them into the rubble of a bombed-out building to take cover. As the planes approached, everyone thought they were taking their last breaths because the pilots could see exactly where they had run to hide. It was going to be a snap to wipe them all out.

The planes came closer, but the rain of bullets stopped. Dad was astonished as he peered out of the rubble and saw each plane tip its wings up and down as it flew over the group. Somehow the pilot of the lone first plane had recognized American POWs, telling the other pilots to do no harm to the larger group. It had been a sorry day for the foolish Nazi guard and a great day for the American POWs. Everyone got what they deserved.

My father wrote in his journal:

That night the guards gave us some black tea. This stuff smelled like hell and tasted worse. I would have never touched it back home. For some reason the guards would not give us any water, only this black tea to drink. It was so bad and we feared it was not what the guards said it was. We had to drink something—the thirst was a never-ending, consistent problem.

They stayed in the vicinity of Chartes for three more days. The Germans kept moving them around, and the POWs were, as always, starving and exhausted from constant walking. They were given very little water and no food for more than four days. The guards once again took care of their own needs; even though food was scarce, they managed to eat enough to kill their hunger pangs. The POWs, on the other hand, were living off the putrid black tea and had resorted to eating fresh grass and insects to survive. Some of the men were complaining to each other that they were developing intestinal trouble and starting to feel sick. Several of the guards finally left the area in search of food and returned a short time later with one loaf of dried out bread, hard as a rock, for thirty-five Germans and Americans to share.

DRIVING THROUGH PARIS

The next day the group moved out, heading for the heart of Paris. This time the guards abandoned the trucks, because most of them were out of gas and broken down. Some of the prisoners were given a long branch with a white flag on top to carry. My dad was one of the lucky ones who received the "stick."

My father wrote this about the experience:

There were a lot of P-38 and P-47 planes flying around. Half of us were carrying white flags. When the planes approached, we were frightened because we always knew the possibility existed that the American pilots would not be able to correctly identify us as prisoners. When they did approach, we'd wave the flags as hard as we could in an effort to be seen.

The Germans marched them well into the early afternoon and then directed them to move into a grove of thick trees. Additional Nazi guards, along with a few more American prisoners, joined their ranks. Well hidden in the bushes were more trucks that had been recently topped off with gas. They loaded everyone up and started the journey to Paris. Many of the POWs were now sick and very weak. The grass, insects, and whatever else they had found to eat had caught up with them. Dad told my mother that he was filthy, and like his fellow prisoners, reeked with body odor. Never in his life had he been dirtier. He hadn't been able to shave in weeks, and his hair was matted and still had blood in it from the terrible day weeks before when he had helped to bury and burn the dead German soldiers.

As they approached Paris, none of the Americans had any idea how large and beautiful the city was. My dad wrote: "Never did I dream we would end up in Paris. I have never in my entire life seen anything like Paris. Seeing this city, I will never forget the beauty of the buildings."

———————

Paris had been under the control of Nazi Germany since 1940. The city's citizens were demoralized, fearful, and oppressed. In early August 1944, the oppression was nearing an all-time high, but the hope that they would soon be free was looming on the horizon. As my father and the other POWs marched into Paris, the U.S. Army was progressing steadily toward the city, and in less than two weeks Paris would be liberated.

The German guards decided to drive the loaded trucks containing the American POWs right to the Arc de Triomphe in the center of the city. The POWs crammed in the back were on display as fallen prisoners for all the French to see. Many of the French cried when they saw the American POWs. The west of France was now occupied by the Americans, and the east was still under the control of the ruthless Nazi regime. Dad's heart was broken; he and the other Americans were the center of attention in a parade no one wanted to see. He had lost his freedom, and the fear of death was ever present. He was miserable and suffering emotionally. But worst of all, he was headed for the interior of Germany, far away from any chance of being rescued by the Allies. He knew his life was going to be like this for a very long time. The momentum was unstoppable. He told my mother that he had to hold back his tears and try to be strong in spite of the situation. Many of the POWs started to cry as they drove through the streets of Paris.

They left the Arc and moved down the spacious Champs-Elysees. The great boulevard harks back to the days of Napoleon. This was the boulevard he paraded down every time he won a great battle. Now the

Americans were being paraded on it as prisoners of war. As the people in the many cafes along the route noticed the convoy of Nazi soldiers and American POWs passing by, they stopped their conversations, stood up, and took their hats off in respect for the Americans. Many left the cafes and approached, praising the Americans and showing concern for them. Some tossed flowers while others offered the POWs food and wine.

When they realized what was happening, the Nazis started pushing the people away from the trucks. The command was given to speed up the motorcade and get out of there. The entire boulevard was quickly filling up with French citizens, and soon the trucks were fully surrounded. The situation had backfired on the Germans as it became clear that the French hated Nazi Germany and its occupation of their beloved country.

The POWs were now suffering from the greatest despair since their capture. Every man knew they were in for the long haul. Dad realized he had three options: die en route to the camp, escape and somehow make it back to the front line, or wait to be liberated from Nazi Germany. Dad rejected the first option, deciding he must survive at all costs. The best choice, he knew, was option three. His determination to be reunited with Eleanore and his family would fuel his determination to make it back home again. Reviewing his situation made him feel better. His goal was to survive by beating the Nazis at their own game.

ILLNESS ON THE ROAD

The crowds dispersed as the Nazi convoy drove out of Paris. They were back in the French countryside and once again focused on their empty stomachs. Some of the POWs were now even sicker with intestinal problems that seemed like the flu. The guards' patience was wearing thin with the many frequent stops. Soon they refused to stop anymore and the sick POWs just gave up and got sick in the back of the truck. After traveling about sixty-five miles they came to the town of Chalons-sur-Marne, which had been devastated by the war. The POWs were becoming sicker by the hour. Fortunately Dad was not sick, but he knew it was only a matter of time.

My father recalled arriving there for my mother: "It was the seventeenth of August 1944. Our living standards had hit a new low. The way we were living was far worse than pigs. Some of the fellows were so weak and sick that they couldn't walk. We were standing in human waste."

Most of the men were now becoming severely dehydrated from vomiting and diarrhea. The water they had been drinking was polluted and full of bacteria from farm run off. The black tea caused severe stomach cramps. The guards were not the least concerned with the physical health of their prisoners, pushing them relentlessly to keep going.

Several of the guards were quietly discussing among themselves that one of the POWs had too many cigarettes in his bulging pants pockets. Dad knew he was about to be discovered. Out of nowhere, the senior guard approached my father and demanded that all his cigarettes be handed over to him immediately. My dad's leveraging power disappeared in an instant. As he dug into his pockets, he was seized with panic as he realized he was relinquishing his lifeline. But Dad retained his composure as he handed his cigarettes over to the guard. He immediately began to shift his thinking to what other bargaining tools he might dream up to make his life easier as a POW.

The guards eventually gave in and stopped at a small abandoned farm. My father explained to my mother that the stench in the back of the trucks had become unbearable for the guards. Driving faster did not eliminate the odor. At the farm some of the men discovered a free-flowing artesian well that was free of bacteria and would become a great benefit to the ailing POWs. The sickest POWs were taken to the barn, where they were given small sips of water to replenish their dehydrated bodies. One of the men found mint growing wild and made a fire to brew hot tea for the men, which settled their rumbling stomachs. The guards stayed away from the POWs, while keeping their guns pointed at them. The POWs were left free to care for themselves.

My dad wrote of this episode in his POW experience: "One of the boys found out they could smoke the black tea! It was far better than drinking it. So we fashioned up some cigarettes and smoked the black tea. It was pretty good."

The Nazis and the POWs stayed in this location for several days. Some of the POWs were feeling better, but others were slipping toward death's door. They could not keep anything down. Water ran through them like a stream, and they were too weak to move.

But on August 23 an unexpected miracle occurred. A lone German truck arrived at camp with gas and supplies for the guards. Also on this truck were several Red Cross boxes with food for the POWs. The German guards, aware of the terrible condition of many of the POWs, handed over the boxes to them. Unfortunately, before relinquishing the food, the Nazis first punctured each can of rations so that nothing could be saved and eaten later. While this upset the men, one of the POWs pointed out that all the food would vanish in one sitting anyway. The first task was to incorporate some of the rations into soup for the extremely ill POWs. This helped save their lives. Tragically, nothing could be done for two of the men, who were dying. In a matter of hours they would be gone. This upset my father horribly, and he spoke about it many times to my mother in his later life.

The first soldier died later that evening and the second on the following day. The guards let the POWs bury them together in a makeshift grave, but would not allow them to mark the grave. Before the burial a POW carefully placed each man's dog tags in his pocket so they could be identified later. Tears and raw emotions prevailed. In the background, my father noticed that the sensitive guard was the only German watching the burial. Looking into the guard's dark brown eyes, Dad could tell he did not agree with the war and its attendant horrors. Dad renewed his personal commitment to somehow figure out how best to deal with these animals. After the burial, rage continued to simmer inside each of the POWs. But there was nothing to be done about it.

It was now more than four weeks since Dad had been captured. Soon the group met up with more American POWs, providing a big mental lift for my father. Among the ten or so new prisoners appeared a familiar face, that of Bert Cottrell. Dad and Bert, who was also from West Virginia, had become friends in basic training but had been separated and placed into different divisions. Now Dad could catch up with Bert and gain a different perspective on the war. Bert was new to the POW life, so Dad gave him a crash course in basic survival and bribery tactics. They were careful not to draw attention to themselves by becoming too chummy. Bert plays a prominent role in my father's war journal.

CROSSING THE BORDER INTO GERMANY

The border crossing was uneventful. Discussions of how to survive slowly turned to Stalag, the prisoner-of-war camp where they knew they were going to end up. Each man was worried about the future of the group as well as his own well-being. Rumors abounded that the Germans were marching Jews out of cities and placing them in concentration camps throughout Germany. Bert told my father that he had fresh information only weeks old that some of these camps were executing the Jewish people at the rate of several thousand a day. This information spread quickly among the POWs, causing them great concern. Anxiety and stress levels increased as their arrival at the prison camp approached. All wondered if they would share the same fate as the Jews or if the Geneva Conventions, the international rules of war, would spare them.

So far, it wasn't looking good. The SS guards had violated almost all of the rules of the Geneva Conventions, including the withholding of food and water, which had led to starvation and death. They had executed soldiers, served up abuse daily, and behaved in indescribably inhumane ways.

The days were getting shorter and the morning air becoming crisp and cold. Fall was arriving in Germany. On sunny days Dad felt warm and secure. But night was an entirely different story. He and his fellow POWs were now freezing at night in their well-worn summer uniforms.

To make matters worse, whenever it rained it was impossible to stay warm. At night the POWs slept close together to share body heat, covering themselves with whatever they could find. Their guards showed no concern whatsoever about their warmth or comfort at night. Sometimes the POWs were allowed to build a fire, sometimes not. The guards remained unpredictable.

———

On September 28 they left the town of Augsburg, Germany, moving closer to the SS Guards' ultimate goal of reaching Stalag VIIA. The men walked quietly most of the time but tensions remained high. The POWs were all very scared, and some of the men began to panic. The guards were slowly increasing their abusive tactics and shows of force. Why the guards had not developed any compassion for their prisoners, especially over the most recent weeks, will always remain a mystery. They were as hostile as ever.

My dad estimated they walked between twenty and thirty-five miles a day over twelve to fifteen hours when not in a truck. It was a horrific ordeal. My mother told me that my father had lost more than thirty pounds from the time of his capture at Mortain until his arrival at the camp. Now, at the worst possible time, my father began to get sick with fever and diarrhea. Becoming weaker with each step, he was also, as usual, starving.

On the evening of the day he became sick, the POWs heard a fleet of German trucks approaching. Two trucks were dropped off, and the rest left for other areas. More than fifty Red Cross boxes were inside one of the trucks. The senior guard gave the order for the POWs to unload the truck and place the Red Cross parcels on the ground. There was food for the guards as well. The starving POWs were beside themselves at the sight of the Red Cross boxes. My father, recalling that evening, said they somehow all found the energy to help unload the truck. The excited men cheered when they were told they could each pick up a box. The guards retreated to their own area, and the POWs gathered in a small grove of trees away from the guards. The POWs started a fire for warmth that night. This was the most relaxed they had ever seen their guards.

Dad was especially grateful for the food, because he knew it was going to help him to feel better. The senior guard announced that they would be arriving tomorrow at their final destination. The smiles disappeared from the faces of the POWs. The nightmare of the last weeks was about to end, to be replaced by an even worse one. With his stomach full for the first time since his capture, Dad's thoughts turned to strategy once again. As he ate, he and the others quietly discussed why they had been given this food now. Was it because their guards wanted them to have enough energy to shine at "show and tell" as they walked into the prison camp? Were they hoping the POWs would suddenly look better than they actually felt? Were they trying to cover up their abuse and neglect? The questions continued between the men.

This was the night that Dad discovered at the bottom of his Red Cross box the YMCA War Log that immediately became so important to him. He would carry it with him all the way back to America.

The Nazi army took about 80,000 American prisoners during World War II. But almost seventy years later not many POW war diaries remain. The YMCA estimates that between 1943 and early 1945, 21,000 War Logs were distributed for American POWs, each accompanied by a cover letter. In the area of Germany where my father was imprisoned 3,000 were distributed, and, at the most, only 400 ever made it back to families in America. Surely many POWs started them, but some were lost, some confiscated by the Nazis and destroyed, and some left behind because of the painful memories they contained.

ARRIVING AT STALAG VIIA

It was mid-morning before the hung-over guards pulled it together to order the POWs to continue on to the prison camp. It had been the longest night of undisturbed sleep the POWs had enjoyed since leaving England. Assembled and ready to go, the Americans were still feeling the benefits of their full stomachs. Right before leaving camp, several of the senior guards began to address the Americans about proper German etiquette and what would be expected of them when they arrived at the Stalag camp.

The POWs wondered why this had suddenly become important. Every American had known they were heading for a Nazi prison camp, despite the senior guards' earlier disinclination to explain this to them.

Gathering the Americans into a single line, the lead senior guard started to speak in English, announcing that they were headed to a prison camp just north of Munich called Stalag VIIA. He also informed the Americans that they were in the custody of Adolf Hitler's army. For their safety, they were to be housed for a time in a military camp that had been specially set up for them. While in the camp, they would be housed and fed, and any medical needs would be promptly taken care of. The guard stressed that good behavior was of utmost importance and that, as in all German prison camps, each of them would be expected to work for fair pay. Any attempt to escape would lead to the severest measures. Escapees, if caught, would be shot immediately. The guard concluded with the following statement:

> When Germany wins the war and the world sees the might and power of the Third Reich, each American who is now a prisoner of Nazi Germany will be returned to the custody of his country after its total and complete surrender to the Third Reich.

Dad was beside himself at hearing this. Could this be true? Was it actually happening? Dad and the others were very alarmed and more concerned than ever about their futures. After all, they'd been given no inkling for the last fifty-four days of how the war was progressing. The morale of the entire group fell to its lowest point up to that time. Suddenly all of them believed it was entirely possible they might remain prisoners for many years to come. A cold shiver ran down my father's spine as he contemplated that the war might drag on for a very long time with no resolution. Dad wondered if anyone in his infantry had finally figured out he'd been taken prisoner by the Germans. Did his parents know? What about Eleanore? These thoughts made him feel bleak, cold, and incredibly sad.

The senior guard's lecture went on for some time. The Germans seemed intent on endless details that nobody cared about. Propaganda permeated the air, becoming a most effective weapon against the men. Dad was stung by how debilitating propaganda could be, especially when there is no other information to compare it to. Everyone theorized that the Nazi guards were trying to break them down even further, rendering them passive and easily controlled upon arrival at the camp. Dad tuned out the guard, ignoring the rest of his message. His mental struggle was already hard enough. But he was unable to stop wondering if it was really possible that the Americans and their allies were now losing the war.

Suddenly one of the guards sprang into action, taking a dog tag away from each of the men. American soldiers are issued two tags when they enter the army. The POWs' tags were going to be turned over to the processing center at the prison camp when they arrived. Giving up one of their dog tags only increased their depression and stress. Years later, with this still fresh in his mind, my dad told my mother:

> Taking our tags was the final blow to all of us. It was like nailing a
> coffin shut—very final, very real. We were all going to prison, and
> nothing was going to change that. We all struggled with this. Some
> of the men had tears in their eyes, some tried to rebel a little, but all
> eventually gave in and gave up their dog tags to the guard.

The Germans announced that they would be traveling on foot for twenty miles. Dad later estimated that it had actually been more like thirty miles. Finally, on September 29, exactly fifty-four days after his capture at Mortain, my father and twenty-five other Americans, under heavy Nazi military guard, walked through the gates of Stalag VIIA, in Moosburg, Germany, and became official prisoners of war of Nazi Germany. The previous eight weeks of tortuous abuse, starvation, and death had taken a toll on each of the men. Dad guessed he'd lost almost forty pounds. Incredibly, his group had traveled the 1,325 kilometers (or 823.31 miles) almost entirely on foot. That they had managed to walk that far and survive under conditions of continuous thirst and starvation was an amazing accomplishment.

It was now late in the evening, and they were directed into a barn located well inside but away from the center of the main camp. Under heavy guard, the camp officials took over, and everyone was told they were not to speak for the rest of the night. Each man found a spot on the floor and began to bed down for the night. While the conditions were harsh, they were much better than the 10' x 10' room into which they'd been crammed at the old fort in France. Dad was actually happier because it was not as cold inside the barn. Of course the men were once again starving, because they'd walked thirty miles since their last meal.

My dad's group was dirty, and the stench of their filthy bodies filled the barn. Fortunately, the German guards couldn't take the smell anymore. Before anyone was allowed to sleep, every man was allowed a hot bath. This was the only luxury they would have, and it was limited to ten minutes each. Dad wrote about his first bath in almost two months: "Best bath ever! Boy did it ever feel good. I had no idea I was capable of getting that dirty."

Dad reported to my mom that the German camp officials had asked the SS guards why their prisoners were so dirty and exhausted compared to the others arriving at the camp. The guards only shrugged their shoulders. At this moment, the word "abuse" was prominent in my dad's mind.

After his bath, Dad had to put back on the same clothes he'd been wearing for weeks. They smelled horrible next to his clean body. He was in shock, wondering just how bad he'd smelled before the bath. The dirt, blood, and stains on his clothes represented his own personal war history on cloth. Dad had dressed in these clothes for the first time in England on June 11, and now it was September 29. He inspected the now-scarred wound on his leg, which had healed just as the medic had predicted. Dad wondered if the medic was still alive or if he had died tragically. He noticed blood stains on his shirt that he knew were not his own, and a wave of sadness swept over him. These were from the endearing little French family he'd loved and buried. His worn and tattered clothes revealed so much about the sorrow and destruction of the past months.

Pushing the bad memories from his mind, Dad tried to think of other things to keep himself from being flooded by unstoppable emotions. He was a survivor who'd completed the first wave of hell. Now he would have to dig into the deepest reaches of his soul to find the courage and strength to make it through this next phase of hell. He was terribly afraid that he wasn't ready for it.

INTERROGATION

The next morning came quickly, with the blaring of the loudspeaker announcing morning roll call. Exhausted, hungry, and emotionally spent, my father slowly opened his eyes to see the shadow of a Nazi guard hovering over him. As the Nazi guard bent over the other sleeping American prisoners, he yelled loudly in German, *"Heraus mit Ihnen Sie niedriges Leben!"* ("Out with you, you low life!").

My father was hearing these demeaning and inflammatory words for the first time on Saturday, September 30, 1944. He would hear them many times again during his imprisonment at Stalag VIIA. The guards kicked and pushed Americans awake, demanding that they move their weary bodies off the floor and out to the yard for morning roll call. Knowing it was Saturday made it only harder for my father. He had been jarred from a dream of past Saturdays in America, days when he'd been happy and carefree. As he pulled himself up off the floor, his body was so stiff and sore that it was a struggle to move outside.

Outside the air was crisp and cool, and Dad and everyone in his group began to shiver from the rapid change in temperature. They were separated from the other prisoners. My father scanned the faces of the hundreds of American prisoners now assembling in the yard. He noticed that many of them looked awful. Their uniforms were torn and tattered, and some had fashioned burlap into coats or hats for themselves. All of them shared the same misery; all were prisoners of Nazi Germany.

Some of the stronger men supported the prisoners who needed assistance walking. Many were having trouble walking or even standing and were relying on the support of their buddies. Soon everyone was assembled in long rows in the yard, and the prisoner count began.

What he was seeing that day horrified my dad. The heartrending reality of POW life was beginning to settle in. Dad would tell my mother later that this roll call would go down as one of the longest ever. It took a lot of time to assemble, count, and verify every prisoner. On this morning several of the men could not be accounted for; also, a very sick American had died in the night. The senior German guards began to scream at the junior guards. Had the missing men abandoned the previous day's work detail outside the camp? Had they pulled off a successful escape the night before? As a soft rain started to fall, every prisoner was now out in the yard as the Nazis searched each hut looking for the two missing men. An hour passed and still no luck. Finally the guards reported to the leaders of the camp that the two Americans were nowhere to be found.

———————

The rain was falling more steadily, and it was very cold. Most of the prisoners were soaked to the bone and shivering violently. Two hours had passed. Dad and his group were carefully watching the events unfolding before them. Now the guard dogs were being pressed into action to catch the scents of the missing men. Dad wondered if they were hiding inside the camp stowed away in garbage scheduled to leave the grounds. The prisoners had become agitated, and many had dropped to the ground in exhaustion. The German guards were pointing their guns and threatening the men, ordering them to remain silent and stand at attention.

The senior guards were furious and taking out their anger on the prisoners in the yard. Finally after almost four hours of standing in the cold rain, the exhausted and hungry men were dismissed and told to return to the barracks. Now the guards turned their attention directly to my father's group. A senior officer ordered all of them back into the central building for processing.

My father talked a great deal to my mother about his first weeks as a prisoner of war. What follows are some of my father's comments, which were told to me by my mother:

> Becoming a prisoner of war is an experience few soldiers endure. It took me a long while to come to grips with it. For a very long time I constantly blamed myself for ending up in that situation. One day in my early months of confinement, I realized that I needed to stop feeling sorry for myself and immediately change my attitude if I was to survive this. Being taken prisoner is neither heroic nor dishonorable. It was an accident, and nothing could have been done to prevent it.
>
> So I made the mental decision that absolutely nothing was going to stop me from surviving. I would survive at all costs, and return home to America.

When I heard these words from my mother, I wanted to cry. I could visualize my father's face as he told my mother what he had been feeling. Lurking in these words were some of the life lessons he had taught me:

"Change your bad attitude when you have one."

"Accidents will happen in life; accept them and figure out how to go around them."

"Whatever you do, never, ever give up your dreams."

————————

Back at Stalag VIIA, as Dad entered the central building, he was pushed along by the guards to hasten his walk. His chest was thumping with nervous anticipation. About to be interrogated by Nazis, he was trying to retain his composure and decide exactly what he wanted to say. Most of the men with him, although equally nervous, had adopted a façade of indifferent toughness, like this was no big deal. Dad knew different. This was going to be a very big deal, and the wrong answers could lead to devastating consequences.

After mulling over countless strategies, Dad decided he'd start with his name, rank, and serial number. His decision was made easier by recalling the barbaric actions of his captors over the last fifty-four days. Anger was beginning to take precedence over his fear, which made him feel better prepared to face a Nazi interrogator. Dad told my mother that he'd had to push his anger to the top of all his other emotions and make himself remember the horrifying things that had happened, in spite of how painful it was to do so. This was going to help him stick to his convictions despite the uncertainty and intensity of the situation. Dad was not going to let himself fold in fear in front of the Nazis. He would never let them see him sweat.

The group was gathered into a large room. A well-worn wooden door was directly in front of them. It was obvious this door had seen much use over the last several years. My father's fifty-four days of captivity had given him a slight psychological edge, because he already knew he could never trust anything said by a Nazi. He was as prepared as he was ever going to be. He decided that if he made it out of this camp alive, he'd certainly plan to tell the army that the training they offered to prepare soldiers for possible capture by the enemy was utterly inadequate.

Dad felt totally abandoned by the army and completely lacking in any training and skills needed for the situation he found himself in. What line of questioning would the Nazis use, my father wondered? Would they speak nicely and try winning him over with a cigarette or two? Or would they be harsh, arrogant, and mean? Dad knew the Nazi interrogators would press him to disclose as many details as possible about the American positions. Any fact he could provide that might ultimately prove useful to the German Army was surely the commandant's goal. After all, if some of the information he provided was beneficial, the commandant might score points with higher-ranking German officials. His mind was in conflict. What should he say? How should he say it?

The door opened. Dressed in full German military uniform, complete with hat, the commandant spoke in perfect English. "Mr. Miller, please come in," he said. His mind full of fear, my father realized he would rather be on the front lines of battle than standing before this Nazi. As he followed the commandant into the room, Dad purposely left the door open behind him. Leaving the door open had been part of his strategy. Dad noticed the absence of any chairs in front of the commandant's wooden desk. It was clear that he would be standing during his questioning. Strangely, there was only one piece of paper on his desk, and it contained scribbled notes in German, which Dad could not read. He saw his army dog tag near the commandant's chair.

"Miller, were you born in a barn?" the commandant said in crisply enunciated English. "Close the door behind you." Dad was amazed at the German's perfect English. Returning to the door, he slowly pushed it closed. Dad was feeling uptight. After a long pause that seemed like an eternity, the commandant finally spoke again in a forceful yet soft voice: "What is your name? Herbert Miller?" My dad said, "Yes," silently wondering why the Nazi had asked his name if he already knew it. Then, just as my dad had predicted, out came the peace offering: cigarettes. My dad was craving a cigarette; he hadn't had one in several days. Fighting off his nicotine fit, he remained neutral and uninterested. The commandant stretched out his hand, offering a cigarette, but Dad declined. "All Americans smoke, why don't you want one?" asked the commandant. My father shook his head. "OK, were you born in the United States?" continued the commandant. My father refused to answer. Turning more serious, the commandant retained a kindly manner. "Mr. Miller," said the commandant, "I must apologize for the conditions you have been experiencing, but I assure you everything will change for the better and you will be very comfortable here once you give me the information I will need to process you." Still my father said nothing.

"Mr. Miller, you must answer me," the commandant continued. "What was your infantry in the army, and when did you land in France?" Dead silence. Both men were now staring at one another. The commandant was becoming agitated. Dad's heart was beating so fast he thought that surely his interrogator could see his chest moving with every beat.

As the stare-off continued between the two men, Dad began to sweat. Now it seemed too hot in the room. He could see that the commandant's patience was quickly eroding into anger. When the questioning resumed, it was much louder in tone. The commandant started firing one question after another:

"Perhaps you did not hear me? Where were you born?"

"How old are you?"

"What did you do in the army?"

Petrified with fear, my father nonetheless stuck to his decision to not give this Nazi commandant any personal information. Without any hesitation, sounding confident and purposeful, he recited the predictable scripted answer he had rehearsed a thousand times over the past fifty-four days as he walked: "My name is Herbert Miller, Private First Class, number 35740482." Before he could finish saying his army serial number, the commandant cut Dad off. "Obviously we have a problem here," he said. "I will ask you these questions once again, and this time I expect answers from you."

"Where were you born?"

No comment from my father.

"How old are you?"

Again, no comment.

"What did you do in the army?"

"My name is Herbert Miller, Private First Class, number 35740482."

By now the commandant was really pissed off. It was obvious to my father that the commandant had been in this exact situation with American prisoners many times before. My father was feeling confident and proud. He was proud to be an American soldier doing exactly what he was supposed to in this situation. The feeling of pride passed quickly, though, and the fear returned. What's next? Dad wondered.

To my dad's surprise, the commandant gave up. His eyes flaring, he slammed both hands down on the desk with enough force to shake the entire room. Springing from his chair, he leaned over the desk and stuck his face in my father's, shouting in German: *"Verlassen Sie mein Büro"* ("Get the hell out of my office").

Suddenly the door sprang open, and two armed German guards came in and escorted Dad away. It was now pouring rain outside the building, and he was immediately ushered outside and placed in the yard with seven other American men. *"Sie stehen hier"* ("You stand here"), one of them said. Dad had been sent to the time-out area for misbehaving prisoners. He was extremely angry now, and hate flooded his mind once again.

The rain continued to pour down on prisoners as they stood under the careful watch of an armed German guard dressed in rain gear and winter clothing. In contrast, the prisoners were wearing their summer uniforms and freezing in the cold fall rain. My father told my mother he had never been so miserable in his whole life. He began to shiver uncontrollably from cold and hunger. Barely holding on, he somehow managed to stand there with the others for almost four hours in the downpour.

I was lucky to find and meet one of my father's most trusted after-the-war friends, John Ciecko. He had also been a POW, in another camp. Because of Ciecko's own first hand POW experiences, my father confided in him many of the horrific stories about what had happened to him at Stalag VIIA. I interviewed John several times, hearing a great many stories about my father's POW experience. Most of them made me cry in sadness. Ciecko explained to me that after arriving at the prison camp my father's rebellious streak emerged in full force. Nothing, not any person or event, was going to break his spirit. He would resist the Nazis at all costs, never giving them any of the critical information they sought from him.

As he stood there freezing and wet in the rain, Dad changed from the easygoing, understanding person of his previous life into a rebellious fighting machine that no one was going to mess with. He vowed to resist all the German's questions, whatever pain it might cause him. This would prove to be a bittersweet decision. He frequently prevailed in many of the situations he was placed in, yet his rebellion had its costs, causing him more hardship, pain, and isolation than most of the other prisoners would ever experience. The word "stubborn" accurately describes my father during his captivity at Stalag VIIA.

It was already dark when the guard told the men to start walking to a hut, where they could stay for the night. The hut, the Nordlager, was for newly arriving prisoners. Here Dad would be given a chance to dry off and get warm. He continued to shiver uncontrollably, finding it very difficult to walk to the Nordlager.

Dad received no medical attention that night or at any other time during his captivity. Many war journals from that time corroborated that this had been a false promise. He often said to my mother and his friend John Ciecko that he could have walked in bleeding profusely with his arms missing and the Nazi guards would not have even looked up. Dad was eventually deloused and given a used, unlined thin wool coat. Rough and scratchy on his skin, it had many small holes and several larger ones located precisely over his heart and stomach. The bigger holes were clearly from bullets. Dad wondered who had owned this coat before him. Had it belonged to a prisoner who'd died in this camp? He decided that the larger holes might have been created by hungry moths. But in reality, he knew he was most likely wearing the coat of a fellow prisoner who had not been lucky enough to survive.

Feeling much warmer in his "new" coat, Dad was given a small piece of black bread and a hot cup of watery soup. It took several hours for his core body temperature to increase, but finally he felt much warmer and more comfortable. Dad stayed in the hut for two days of quarantine to make sure that he had been debugged and would not infect the others in the camp. This was pretty ironic, because Stalag VIIA was permeated with lice, fleas, and bugs. It was only a matter of time before every prisoner encountered them. POWs learned to survive with bugs.

After two days, Dad was issued his Stalag VIIA dog tag, bearing his prisoner number, 85 464. And he was given the permanent hut assignment of 30A. The Germans also returned his army dog tag taken from him days earlier. Hut 30A was exclusively for American soldiers who'd been captured by the Nazis. It was crowded, dismal, dark, and cold, but Dad was happiest inside because it was slightly warmer and drier than the outside. Still, with no heat and very little light, it was a very depressing place, especially with the winter months approaching.

Dad's war possessions now consisted of the following: his original summer uniform with several tears in it from the shrapnel that had ripped into his leg, his American and Stalag dog tags, his P-38 can opener, my mom's picture taped inside his undershirt, the relic he'd picked up in Mortain, his YMCA War Log that he kept in his pants, and his "new" old scratchy woolen coat loaded with holes.

As he entered his new home for the first time, Dad found the conditions inside truly challenging. The men already there were starving, and it clearly showed in their thinner-than-normal bodies. The place reeked with the type of stench associated with person overload. The barracks, or huts, as they were called, were drafty rectangular wooden buildings with no insulation. In some places you could see through the cracks in the walls to the outside. Each building was divided into two sections, A and B, with a central room that was used for washing and eating. In that central room was one water faucet and a hand pump that only dispensed ice-cold water. All of the POWs slept on triple-deck wooden bunks with gunnysack mattresses filled with hay or excelsior and loaded with fleas and lice. The huts were originally designed to hold 180 men tightly. When my dad arrived, hut 30A was occupied by more than 225 men. Because of overcrowding, Dad's bunk was the top of a table. Unless someone died, escaped, or was transferred, this was going to be his bed for a very long time.

Top: Young Herbert Miller in West Virginia; Right: Miller, his sister Marlene (on his lap), his sister Phyllis, and his brother, Hank.

Clockwise from top left: Herbert Miller shortly after his release from Stalag XVIIIC in May 1945; the photo of Eleanore Kurowski Miller taped inside his T-shirt next to his heart and wore throughout the war; navy seaman John McGuckin, who ferried soldiers to Omaha Beach in an LCI on D-Day; Omaha Beach on D-Day; the house where Miller grew up in Warwood, West Virginia; Eleanore Kurowski with Tilley Dunbek, the friend who introduced her to her West Virginia cousin Herbert Miller in 1943.

Clockwise from above: The city of Mortain at the time of the Battle of Mortain; a view of the thirteenth-century Chapelle Saint-Michel from the bottom of Hill 314 near Mortain; the inside of the severely damaged chapel, where Herbert Miller discovered the relic he would carry with him for the rest of the war.

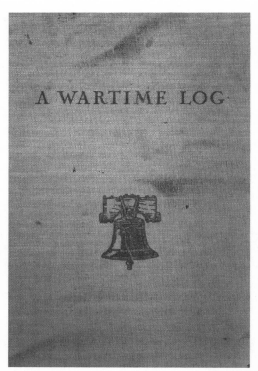

Top: Herbert Miller's journal, created by the YMCA and distributed to POWs by the Red Cross; Right: The opening page of the journal inscribed by Miller.

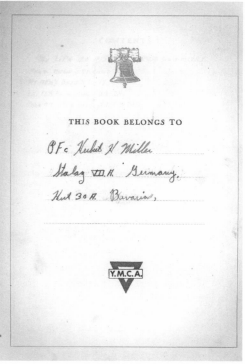

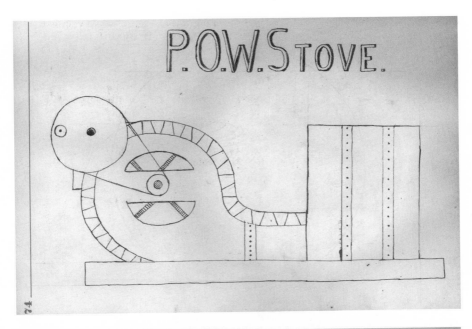

Top: Herbert Miller's drawing of a POW stove from his war journal; Bottom: Stalag VIIA in Moosburg, Germany.

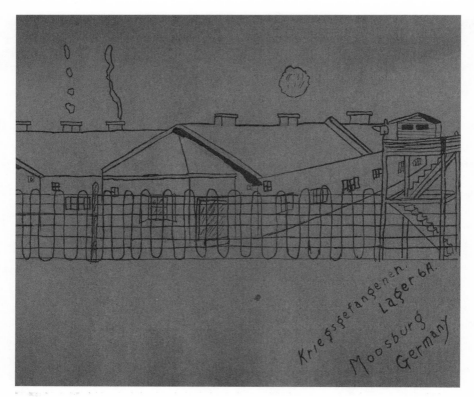

Kriegsgefangenen. Lager 6A. Moosburg Germany

Gefangenenalltag im Lager

THE FOLLOWINGS ARE DATES OF BOMBING.

OCTUBER — 24   LIGHT. RAID ... NIGHTRAID.

NOVEMbER   4   VERY HEAVY .... DAY RAID

NOVEMbER   16   VERY HEAVY .... NIGHT RAID 2: AM.

NOVEMbER   29   VERY HEAVY .... NIGHT RAID 7-30 - 1.30

DECEMbER   17   VERY HEAVY .... NIGHT RAID 12:00.

JANUARY   7   VERY HEAVY .... NIGHT RAID

JANUARY   15   VERY HEAVY --- NIGHT RAID

JANUARY   21   VERY HEAVY ---- DAYRAID.

ONE TEN RERCENT OF MUNCHEN IS STILL
STANDING AND THAT IS FAR OUT SKIRTS OF
TOWN. I BELIVE IF THEY KEEP UP MÜNCHEN
WILL BE ALL KAPUT.

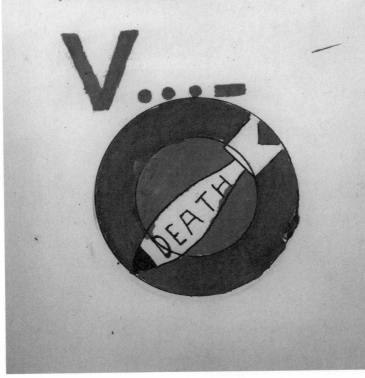

Clockwise from top left: Herbert Miller's drawing of Stalag VIIA from his war journal; Miller's log, from his war journal, of air raids in Munich from October 1944 to January 1945; POWs sunning themselves at Stalag VIIA.

Left: A collage of labels from the food Stalag VIIA POWs ate at Christmas in 1944, from Herbert Miller's war journal; Above: Heinz, the caring Nazi guard who formed a strong bond of friendship with Miller.

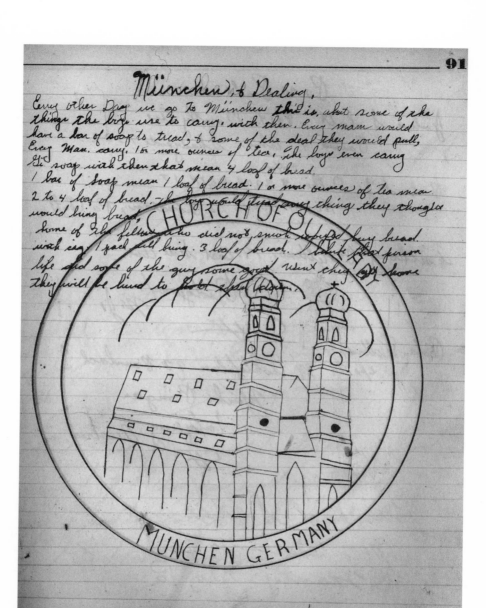

Münchens, & Dealing.

Every other Day we go to München this is what some of the things the boys use to carry with them. Every man would have a bar of soap to trade, & some of the deal they would pull, Every Man carry 1 or more ounces of tea. The boys even carry the soap with then that mean 4 loaf of bread. 1 bar of soap mean 1 loaf of bread. 1 or more ounces of tea mean 2 to 4 loaf of bread. The boys would trade any thing they thought would bring bread. Some of the fellows who did not smoke would buy bread with cig. I said all bring 3 loaf of bread. I think that person life did some of the guy some good went they get home they will be hard to get along with.

CHURCH OF OUR LADY

MÜNCHEN GERMANY

Above: A page from Herbert Miller's war journal, which describes the bartering the POWs did for food while on work detail in Munich and includes a drawing of the Church of Our Lady near the bombed-out areas where they cleared rubble; Right: the charcoal portrait of Eleanore Kurowski that POW Miles created on Christmas Day 1944.

Drawing by POW Miles

Top: POWs at Stalag XVIIIC near Markt Pongau in Austria; Right: During his second escape attempt, Herbert Miller sketched from memory in his war diary his fellow POWs around the POW stove at Stalag VIIA; Above: Miller's U.S. Army dog tags, his Stalag VIIA dog tag, and his P-38 can opener.

STOVES

Camp Lucky Strike near Le Havre, France, was one of many "cigarette" camps where POWs were sent until they were able to go home.

This photo is labeled "France 1945" and it was found in an envelope marked "Bert." It is of Herbert Miller, who is probably with his pal Bert Cottrell in France after their release from the POW camp in Austria.

Left: Eleanor and Herbert Miller on their wedding day, August 25, 1945. Above: The Millers on their son Robert's wedding day, October 18, 1980.

Photo Anne Sarrazin

Photo Robert H. Miller

on the occasion of the 65th anniversary of the landing in Normandy

The Honorable
Barack Obama
President of the
United States of America

His Excellency
Nicolas Sarkozy
President of the
French Republic

request your presence
on Saturday 6 June 2009 at 3:00 p.m.
at the Normandy American Cemetery and Memorial in Colleville-sur-Mer.

Clockwise from top left: Robert Miller and Noel Sarrazin in Mortain, France, in a restored U.S. Army jeep exactly like the one Herbert Miller drove before his capture by the Nazis near Mortain, France, in August 1944; Robert Miller's invitation from the White House to the Sixty-fifth Anniversary of D-Day commemoration ceremony in Colleville-sur-Mer, France, in June 2009; The Normandy American Cemetery in Colleville-sur-Mer, with two U. S. Navy ships anchored off-shore; Former 30th Infantry soldier Frank Towers in Mortain in June 2009 to receive France's Legion of Honor Medal.

Photo taken in 2008 of Chapelle Saint-Michel, near Mortain, France.

PRISON CAMP LIFE

My father lay motionless on top of his makeshift bedding, his lifeless eyes staring up at wooden beams that made the barracks seem like the inside of an old barn. Fleas kept jumping into his field of vision, interrupting his view. Every bed in the camp was infested with bugs. Ignoring the fleas and their bites, he let his mind wander away from the dreary day and his ongoing misery. He focused on the unique grain pattern of the wooden beams, which reminded him of a human face. Soon he was recalling his childhood friends, identical twins Tim and Jim Nodurft, who had served together in this awful war. The twins had died in a foxhole during Operation Cobra.

Overwhelmed by sadness, Dad took his gaze away from the beams and found a new focal point, a small hole in the ceiling. He tried to think about Eleanore, his parents, and happier times, but his mind kept returning to the most disgusting place on earth, Stalag VIIA.

He began to think about the looming winter. The days were becoming noticeably shorter. The loss of daylight and slowly falling temperatures added to the suffering of the prisoners. Staying put inside the squalid hut was now a better choice than venturing out to face rain, wind, and cold. Occasionally the sun would peek out from behind the clouds, casting its brilliance down upon the men. This was a bittersweet reminder of summer days gone by.

Scanning the interior of the dimly lit hut, Dad observed its flimsy construction. Cold air permeated the paper-thin walls of the structure. The raw wood, combined with the stench of men who hadn't bathed in months, created a pungent, musty smell like that of rotting wood. Dad and his fellow prisoners now called this place home.

It had been over two months since his capture by the Germans and Dad was depressed, unable to even muster the will to write in his journal. He was also starving from the lack of nourishing food. He wondered constantly if his parents and Eleanore knew about his capture. He had been allowed to send letters to them shortly after he arrived at the camp. But he still didn't know if his letters had ever arrived in America. Dad also questioned whether the army knew about his capture, because it had taken a long time for his POW information to reach the Red Cross. In his mind he was still just a missing man to the army and his family. How agonizing this must be for them, he thought.

Dad recalled a confrontation he'd had with a German guard at the beginning of his imprisonment. Violating a strict camp rule, he'd relieved himself outside the hut instead of using the foul-smelling latrines overflowing inside. Dad had actually thought he was doing the Germans a favor by not adding to the mess. The guard had hit him in the head with the back end of his rifle, pushing my dad down into his own excrement. His mind and sight were briefly impaired as he struggled to regain awareness and composure. Now he had a gash at the back of his skull. After that Dad followed the camp rule, using the latrines inside the barracks whatever their condition.

Dad thought about what he'd learned about the camp since his arrival. When he was outside, he could see straight through the many barbed-wire fences that separated and defined the camp, creating mini-prisons. Stalag VIIA's prisoners were a global melting pot. The Germans tried to keep the nationalities segregated by country of origin in these separate compounds. But they were running out of space fast. Every day more prisoners arrived to be unloaded into the yards. A soldier captured by Nazi Germany would most likely wind up here in Stalag VIIA, the largest prisoner-of-war camp in Europe. Dad observed crude communication through simple gestures and sign language between different nationalities in adjoining yards. It isn't hard for a hungry prisoner to understand the sign language for "Do you have any food?"

Stalag VIIA was so large that my father could not see to the end of it from his hut. When he looked beyond his own fenced compound, he saw a consistent pattern of guard towers that likely surrounded the entire camp. Each tower was equipped with machine guns the Nazi guards in the towers were prepared to use. The perimeter of the camp was surrounded by two twelve-foot-high barbed-wire barriers spaced about twenty feet apart. Inside this no-man's land, tightly coiled barbed wire was evenly laid in long rows on the ground, making it unlikely that a prisoner would ever get through.

As far as Dad could see in every direction were straight rows of drab gray buildings that resembled neighborhoods in the small towns near Wheeling where he had grown up. Dad often mentioned to my mother that the neighborhoods at his camp were a constant and depressing reminder of the better life he'd left behind before he entered the war.

Guards with dogs constantly patrolled the camp. Dad observed that the Germans preferred three types of dogs: the German Shepherd, known for its strength and intelligence; the alert and loyal Doberman Pinscher; and the powerfully built Mastiff. Dad often walked alone to the edge of the fence inside his compound, arriving at the "safe" area before a German guard raised his rifle and placed him in its sights. Trained to attack, the Mastiffs would go wild, straining at their leashes. Dad and the other prisoners quickly became very savvy, learning just how close they could get to the fence before a guard took aim.

My father would often glance over at the solitary confinement camp called the *Sonder barack,* just outside the main gate. This was a special detention area for all the prisoners who had escaped from Stalag and been recaptured. Dad was always drawn to this area—it haunted him and he paid a visit almost every day. The men inside the Sonder barack were even more miserable and starved than the rest of the inmates. The

Nazis withheld food and provided just enough water to keep a man alive. Two weeks in the Sonder barack would change a soldier's attitude and give him new reasons to conform to the rules of the prison. Most eventually accepted their fate and never tried to escape again.

Feeling sorry for these men, Dad started saving food scraps. When the guard wasn't looking, he'd toss a morsel of bread over the tall fence. Dad got away with this several times, watching those inside the Sonder barack run to grab the food scraps off the ground. He could see the gratitude in their eyes and hand gestures. No words were ever spoken between them.

———

Staring listlessly at the ceiling above his bed, Dad continued to think about all of this. He struggled to breathe, because inhaling caused a sharp pain in his side. A familiar anger began to rise in him as he remembered his second rifle butt. It had happened the day before while visiting the Sonder barack area. Just as Dad's morsel of bread made it over the fence, a guard's rifle butt had come out of nowhere. As Dad grimaced in pain on the ground, he saw another guard, inside the Sonder barack, racing toward the scrap of food with his dog. The guard quickly placed his foot over it, crushing it into the dirt.

The guard who'd skillfully smashed his rifle butt into Dad's side was now hovering over him with his gun drawn. Forcing the gun muzzle into his cheek, the guard shouted in German: *"Nien ließ dieses wieder geschehen"* ("Never let this happen again").

Even after suffering the pain and humiliation of being caught, Dad couldn't promise himself that he'd never smuggle food to the prisoners of the Sonder barack again. Why do I have these strong feelings? he wondered. In his mind Dad divided the prisoners into two groups: the conformists and the doers. The conformists were the largest group, accepting their fate and hoping for the best. They offered no resistance to the guards, doing their time and waiting for liberation. The doers, on the other hand, were free spirits who refused to be worn down. These men knew how to manipulate the system. Some doers actually succeeded in making things better for themselves. Sometimes the junior guards were so taken aback by the actions of these doers that they'd give in just to see what might happen. Doers took these risks to survive or improve their conditions.

Dad continued to wrestle with his thoughts. He theorized that the guards at Stalag VIIA also fell into these two groups. The doers were the staunch Hitler loyalists, SS Guards who made life unspeakable for anyone other than a Nazi. The conformists had been forced into the military by the Nazis and fervently wished they were somewhere else. They most likely didn't agree with the Third Reich but believed they had no choice.

Now it was starting to make sense, he thought. Freedom was the only goal that made any sense for the guys in solitary confinement. Some were unlucky and would be killed for the risks they'd taken. The bottom line, my dad decided, was that everyone in solitary confinement was a doer. Conformists were nowhere to be found in the Sonder barack.

Dad speculated that every man in the camp must have thought at one time or other about escaping. Why did some men try to escape when others would never attempt it? All of these thoughts were smoldering inside him when he felt the hand of his friend Bert Cottrell wiggling his leg. "Herbert, Herbert, are you OK?" he called out. "What's the matter with you? Can't you hear me?" Dad came out of his reverie, slowly moving his battered body from the bunk. He realized that his rib pain was definitely for real. "I can't believe those Nazi bastards did this to you!" said Cottrell. "Are you going to be OK?" Holding his breath, Dad struggled to his feet. He looked into his friend's eyes and said, "I am now."

Over the next several days, Dad's attitude improved and his spirits revived. He was no longer feeling sorry for himself, and his depression began to lift. Dad's body was also on the mend, with the pain from the rifle butt injury diminishing. A break in the weather allowed the men to shed their overcoats at midday and enjoy the sunshine as they soaked up the last warm moments of fall.

HEINZ, THE GOOD NAZI GUARD

O ne day Dad caught sight of a familiar German face. It was the Nazi guard who, on the fateful night of August 6, had pressed the barrel of his gun into my dad's back, announcing that he was now a prisoner of Nazi Germany. Dad had quickly discerned that this guard was different from the rest. Soft-spoken, he appeared highly educated and polished, emanating kindness and understanding. He also took an interest in the well-being of the American prisoners. It was clear to my dad and the other POWs that this guard wanted nothing to do with Nazi Germany or its army.

The guard approached my father, greeting him with a slight smile. Speaking perfect English, he glanced around cautiously, saying in a low voice, "Hello, my name is Heinz." Surprised, my dad smiled back, replying, "My name is Herbert." Heinz said he knew my father's name from the interrogation records and remembered him from their long journey together. "You are the one who is always hungry," Heinz said. My father replied, "Yes I am, and I'm very hungry now."

Heinz was now responsible for guarding the area in which my father and the other American POWs were imprisoned. After their brief conversation Heinz began to walk on, trying to avoid scrutiny. "I'll see what I can do for you," were his parting words to my father. Stunned, my father mouthed "thank you" as Heinz disappeared around the corner. Feeling optimistic for the first time in weeks, Dad returned to his hut and drifted off to sleep, hoping to take his mind off his hunger and his injured side.

Dad's meager daily ration of food provided little in the way of either nutrition or calories. The typical POW was always exhausted, cold, and in a daze. Dysentery and intestinal problems plagued everyone. It was not a pleasant experience.

The next day at 5 a.m. the men were rousted out of bed and told to assemble in the main courtyard for morning inspection. Groggy and sore, Dad managed to pull himself together and get to the yard. After the daily count, if no one was missing or dead, work details would be organized for the day.

Dad's side was still too sore for him to go on a work detail. Due to Heinz's kindness and concern, Dad was able to recuperate for several more days. Breakfast, a cup of black liquid resembling coffee, came after roll call. With luck, it might even be warm. Sometimes thick black bread made up of 50 percent sawdust was also served to the POWs. At noon a watery concoction appeared, swimming with often-rotten potatoes, which the Germans called soup. Again, with luck, Dad might be the one to receive the lone green bean in his soup. Supper consisted of a one-inch-thick slice of rock-like brown or black "sawdust" bread and one small boiled potato. Once a week Dad received a ration of meat, either horse meat or bologna, depending on what was available. Often the meat was spoiled, adding further to the miseries of prison life. Because of the "Sawdust Diet," as my father liked to call it, he continued to lose weight every week. The men would sporadically receive Red Cross food boxes, sharing one between two men. Begging, bartering, and occasionally stealing food were the norm.

WORK DETAIL IN MUNICH

The first icy grip of winter was now blasting away at the camp. Often it was colder inside the hut than out. During the day the air outside would warm up, while the cold air stayed trapped inside the huts. My father finally felt recovered enough to go out on work details with the other POWs. Leaving camp to work was a bittersweet experience. Every POW who went out received a daily allotment of not-so-nourishing food. At noon, as a bonus, each soldier was given two large glasses of German beer, which was easier to get than fresh water. The Germans hoped the calories in the beer would keep their charges working at a steady pace. Often the POWs brought Red Cross soap and cigarettes to trade with civilians for real bread. American cigarettes were like gold, and even the German guards would offer food or special considerations in exchange for POWs' cigarettes. Swapping one small bar of Red Cross soap could yield up to four loaves of fresh bread from German citizens.

To go on work detail, the POWs had to get up very early to leave the camp and be packed like sardines into cattle cars for the ride to Munich. My mother remembered my father telling her appalling stories about this experience. "Your dad remembered how the rail cars were always locked. A small wooden barrel was in the corner of the box car for the prisoners to relieve themselves in. With every trip, it did not take long for this barrel to start overflowing with human waste."

Dad makes clear on page sixty-seven of his journal how he felt about his many trips to Munich during his incarceration. On that page he kept track of all the major bombing and strafing campaigns by the American forces. I believe the many near-death experiences he survived in Munich altered his life forever. Page sixty-seven is the only one in the entire journal that he wrote in bright red marker.

Mom told me that these events in Munich kept resurfacing in the horrible dreams he had later in life. My father suffered guilt when my sister and I were growing up from his inability to handle large crowds, excessive noise, air shows, and fireworks. My father couldn't go near events that brought back the terrors of his past.

The winter of 1944–1945 was one of the coldest and snowiest on record. With the outside temperature in the single digits and an extreme wind chill from the movement of the well-ventilated train, the temperature inside the rail cars could plummet to well below zero. On one trip to Munich my dad and the others suffered frostbite as they huddled together to stay warm. The trip sometimes took over four hours because of strafing by the Allied pilots. It was a very dangerous situation. Finally, according to Mom, the Nazi guards on the train wised up and let the prisoners paint the letters "POW" in white paint on top of the rail cars to stave off the American pilots.

Unfortunately, on two separate occasions over a four-month period, my father's train was hit by friendly fire, and innocent American POWs lost their lives. When this happened, getting back to the prison camp could take several days while the rails were replaced and repaired.

On the train to Munich, shortly after he arrived at Stalag VIIA, Dad was injured for the second time in the war, narrowly escaping with his life, as shrapnel from an exploding bomb grazed his right leg. He had just made a new friend at Stalag several days earlier, and this soldier would not end up so lucky. As they boarded the train, the two men were separated by the guards. Dad was placed in the last boxcar at the rear of the train, and his friend was sent to the most forward boxcar directly behind the engine.

The train left Moosburg and began to make its way toward Munich. In the meantime, American planes were busy bombing the hell out of Munich. Seeing Dad's unmarked train far below, American forces thought it was a German train and aimed their bombs accordingly. The deafening low whine of descending aircraft sent a cold chill through everyone on the train. There would be no escaping the tomb they were now in. American forces knew to target the engine, in order to disable the entire train. Hearing the massive explosions, Dad and the others at the back feared the worst; terror filled the inside of the boxcar. Many of the men began to pray as the bombs came closer. Some cried and others, like my father, were paralyzed with fear. The bombs vaporized Dad's friend at the front of the train as well as many other POWs.

As the train ground to a halt, the bucket in the corner of Dad's boxcar, filled to the brim with human waste, spilled over, covering most of the men with its contents. A number of the men were thrown into the walls of the boxcar and injured. No one could escape the boxcar until the Nazis came and undid the padlocks. Finally Dad and the others were freed. But they were forced at gunpoint to work well into the night to restore the tracks, with no food and American bombs landing all around them. Later that night, they were ordered to take up residence in a bombed-out building among the rubble and find a spot to sleep. This extremely traumatizing experience resulted in lifelong emotional scars for my dad.

The next day was even worse. Now the POWs were moved to what was left of a group of buildings near a Catholic church and told to clear the dead out of the rubble and pile the bodies and body parts on a cart for burial. The dead bodies were endless and included those of children. The POWs were gagging, becoming sick from the stench of the dead. The men already reeked from the human waste that had spilled in their boxcar the previous day.

Many of the Nazi guards laughed as bombers approached the area, referring to American bombs as "golden eggs." Nazis just didn't care if American POWs were hit with friendly fire.

My father traveled to Munich on work detail for over six months. The horror of what he experienced seems indescribable to me. The POWs working in Munich were in danger every moment of dying from Allied bombing runs. Dad lost several friends in Munich as they worked digging out bomb debris from earlier raids. After the work detail was over, usually about 5 p.m., everyone would be rounded up and packed back into the boxcars for the return trip to the camp. They were given an evening meal when they got back. This was the incentive the Germans dreamed up to get as many POWs out on work detail as possible: a slightly higher volume of food and the bonus of beer for work performed. As my father used to say to my mother, "Die or eat." Every day was a choice.

POW SOUP AND DAD'S MOTHBALLS

Winter had now arrived with full force. Temperatures were well below freezing, and snow was piling up in the camp yard. It was Thanksgiving week, and the American holiday would not be a holiday for the men. On a Sunday morning, shivering almost uncontrollably, Dad opened his eyes and found the hole in the roof that was his focal point. It was dead quiet inside his hut. All the men were freezing and silently waiting for the roll call to begin. Dad's stomach was growling, and he'd woken up with a slight headache that was steadily increasing. The first thoughts in his mind, as always, were of Eleanore and his family. Certainly they must know I am a prisoner of war, he thought. He wished he knew what had arrived first: his letters or the telegram from the army informing them he was missing in action and was now a prisoner of war. Dad realized that the army would inform his parents first because they were listed as his next of kin and he was not yet married to Eleanore. He hoped his letters to Eleanore had made it through, though, because it would be comforting for her to learn in his own handwriting that he was alive.

Roll call began and the men jumped out of their beds, gathered whatever clothing they could put their hands on, and headed outside. It was snowing, cold, and very damp. Thank God nobody had escaped or died the night before. Today's roll call would be quick and relatively painless. Afterward the German guard Heinz approached my father and others nearby to quietly announce that he had a surprise for them. First, he said he needed to inspect their barracks. Speaking loudly in German, and making gestures and gun movements for all the other German guards to see, he rounded the men up at gunpoint and marched them inside for the inspection. Once inside, he lowered his gun and spoke quietly to my father and the others, explaining that he had beef bones in his pockets that could be made into soup. My dad told my mother that some of them danced with glee. Dad was almost in tears as he accepted the soup bones from his German friend. They were going to make a nourishing soup from the German guards' table scraps. To their surprise, the bones even had plenty of meat on them. The protein would help them survive.

Heinz told the men that the senior guards always wasted food because their cooks made too much, and all the extras went in the garbage and were taken out of the camp and burned. Junior guards weren't given food that good, although what they ate was much better than POW food, and they could have their fill. He told the POWs to take the scraps and not tell anybody.

The grateful men took the table scraps and placed them under a floorboard on top of my father's journal. To this day the journal bears the stains from those table scraps. Heinz ordered everyone outside, gathering up the group at gunpoint and marching them out. It looked like a normal day at Stalag VIIA. Heinz lit a cigarette, quietly telling my father that the British in the next barracks over had devised a simple stove made from a large can with a crank. When cinders from the stove were placed in the can, turning the handle increased the heat, making a cookstove. The stove design, explained Heinz, was quickly being adopted and used all over the camp. Heinz told them he knew where to get them a crank for a trade of twenty-five cigarettes. All they would need, he said, was the can, a floorboard, and a few nails. My father told him to get the crank and he and the other POWs would collect the cigarettes. Dad also told Heinz that his friend Bert had several empty cans they could use, along with a board and some nails from the hut. Heinz threw down his cigarette and smashed it in the snow, saying he'd be back with the crank later that day.

Back in the hut, the men were excited, their mouths already watering at the anticipation of homemade soup. Bert had brought the can and was now busying himself with prying up a floorboard that would not be missed. Along with the board came the nails needed to fasten down the can. The men worked at modifying the can to fit tightly against the board, and small rocks were collected and placed in the can so hot cinders would not burn through the board. The cigarettes were collected, and Dad added a few more to show his appreciation. With great anticipation, they all waited for Heinz to return with the crank.

Later that day Heinz stormed into the hut with his gun drawn. This startled and alarmed the POWs, but after Heinz closed the flimsy door he apologized for his rude entry, explaining it had been necessary to keep down any suspicions about what he was up to. The relieved men gathered around Heinz as he pulled two cranks from his pockets. They cheered quietly and patted Heinz on the back. He explained that he'd convinced the German guard who was responsible for guarding the British to give him two cranks, telling him he'd get thirty cigarettes in return.

Stalag is all about bartering, explained Heinz. The British soldiers who made these devices were so hooked on cigarettes that there were never enough to go around. When the craving started and their Red Cross parcels hadn't arrived yet, someone could practically get the shirt off their backs in exchange for just one cigarette. Heinz told them this was how he had managed to come up with two cranks. Dad had the cigarettes in his hand and was very happy he'd already decided to give him extras. Heinz put the cigarettes in his pocket, wished everyone well, and left the hut.

The POWs set to work, and pretty soon were starting to put together the second stove. Two of the POWs were leery of Dad's new German friend. In a state of panic, they worried they'd be caught and thrown into isolation. Most were happy, though, seeing a big benefit for all of them. Dad reminded everyone that he had sized up Heinz in August. They'd already benefited many times, he said, from Heinz's kindness

and concern over the past months. Dad emphasized that back in September on the march to Moosburg Heinz had placed himself in major
jeopardy. He'd convinced the senior guards not to place the POWs in
unmarked German trucks and send them all to the front of the line,
where they would certainly have become the target of American bombs.
Heinz would have been shot on the spot if the other guards had suspected he was in sympathy with the Americans.

"What in the hell do we have left?" Dad told his fellow POWs. "I'm
for taking every advantage we can find to make our lives easier inside
this hellhole. I personally will not roll over and die because of these Nazi
bastards," he continued. "I would rather die trying than not to have tried
at all. Now, who wants to eat soup later? Let's get focused and take advantage of the situation."

The message landed positively. Everyone now wanted to be friends
with Heinz. Dad's stubbornness and confidence was back, and he was
taking the actions necessary to improve his day-to-day life. If the others agreed with him, he said, they were more than welcome to come
along for the ride. If they didn't agree, it was their choice, and it would
be respected.

After boiling the hell out of the meat and bones, and adding scraps
of potatoes they'd traded for in another hut, the soup was complete. The
POW stove worked great. The soup tasted wonderful and was a great
mental lift, making the cold, dark night more tolerable. Soon others in
the hut could smell the gourmet feast and were asking questions. The
bones would be cooked again and Bert created a small area under the
floor to keep the precious table scraps hidden from view. Every man in
the hut was now on the lookout for anything that could be transformed
into a heart-warming pot of soup.

Thanksgiving Day arrived, and it was just another work day for everyone in Stalag VIIA. The Nazis were certainly not going to acknowledge
an American holiday, with the exception of Heinz. Because the snow
was piling up and the temperature at twelve degrees, the Nazis decided

to cancel all work details for the day. Most likely they had no desire to stand outside in the freezing cold overseeing the POWs.

Late in the morning Heinz rounded everyone up for the usual loud, gun-waving hut inspection. Once safely inside, he delivered a pile of still-warm chicken bones to the men. His pockets were almost overflowing. "Happy Thanksgiving," announced Heinz. Astonished, they all thanked him from the bottom of their hearts for the table scraps and for remembering this special American holiday.

Bert and Dad smiled at one another as they contemplated what they were going to do with those chicken bones. For his kind generosity, Heinz was offered a pile of cigarettes by Bert. The bones were quickly hidden in the secret storage area. But Bert had detected a strong chicken smell emanating from Heinz's coat pockets. If the German guard dogs caught a whiff of him, he would be in serious trouble. Gravely concerned for Heinz's safety, the men tried to come up with a way to camouflage the smell and trick the dogs.

Heinz was now visibly shaken. It was a miracle he hadn't been discovered on his way to the hut by the guard dogs. Even the dogs were kept underfed, because it made them aggressive and edgy. In a stroke of luck, Dad remembered the mothballs he'd collected from a bombed-out house in Munich and stashed under the floorboards. When he brought them back to the hut, most of the POWs hadn't understood they were an effective deterrent against fleas, lice, and bedbugs. Dad had put a small cache of mothballs inside his bedding, effectively reducing his infestation problem. Now Dad divided up the mothballs, and the men started rubbing them inside Heinz's pockets to kill the chicken smell. Pretty soon he smelled like mothballs. Heinz and the POWs had come full circle in friendship—all were working together now for one common goal. My father told my mother that Heinz had tears in his eyes that day. He couldn't stop thanking the men. Bert was the first to respond, saying, "This is what an American Thanksgiving is all about."

As Heinz left the hut, Dad and the others peered cautiously through the irregular glass windows, watching as he carefully negotiated the yard. Heinz tried to stay clear of guard dogs, but he was about 200 yards from the hut when a guard with a Doberman Pinscher at his side waved Heinz down. Inside the hut all eyes were on the dog. Several minutes passed, tension and uncertainty hovering in the air. The POWs knew the mothballs had worked when the Doberman started pulling the guard away from Heinz. A sigh of relief spread throughout the hut. No one ever again made a comment about my father's mothballs smelling bad. The men spent the rest of the day sharing Red Cross boxes and making chicken soup. How thankful they were to be celebrating Thanksgiving together, in spite of their dismal status as prisoners of Nazi Germany.

MUNICH DEALING AND STEALING POTATOES

The misery of POW life grew worse over the next several weeks. Every day more American prisoners arrived at the camp, and the huts were now overflowing with prisoners. By mid-December the population of my dad's hut had reached 250 men. With outside temperatures now in single digits, the windows of his hut were covered with frost from the condensation created by so many prisoners breathing inside. Food was getting scarcer, and the daily soup was full of rotten potatoes and vegetables.

My father and six other men were now sharing one Red Cross parcel every two weeks. Because of this, many of the men, including my father, jumped at the opportunity to leave the camp for work detail. Working away from Stalag meant a midday meal for the men, which helped to quell their constant hunger pangs. It was a two-edged sword, however, because they burned even more calories doing hard physical labor. More often than not, by evening they were once again starving. The POWs could never build a reserve of calories or body fat. Dad's weekly weight loss continued.

The Nazi regime took advantage of the war situation, enforcing the Geneva Convention stipulating that lower-ranking POWs like my father could be put to work as needed. Dad was placed on *Arbeitskommandos*, or work units, where he was sent to labor at farms or made to clear the massive rubble in Munich from Allied bombings. While on work duty

Dad and his buddies often met sympathetic German civilians, who gave them food. Dad learned quickly that if he brought cigarettes and soap with him from his Red Cross box he could trade them for bread and cheese. During most of the war German civilians had little or no access to soap or cigarettes. This "Munich dealing," as the POWs called it, was a critical part of work detail.

Obtaining food illegally could cause serious problems for a POW if he wasn't careful. My father recalled for my mother one instance when his attempts to get something to eat almost got him killed. A particular Nazi guard was well known for using his bayonet against anyone that irritated him. He'd kill a POW and then blame it on American bombs.

———————

One day Dad and several others were pulled away from the morning lineup and moved under guard to an area just outside the main gate. They were told to start putting a shipment of potatoes into long, straw-filled trenches. After the trenches were filled, they were ordered to cover the potatoes with another layer of straw followed by a layer of dirt.

The Americans were hungry, as usual, and the smell of the potatoes was more than they could handle. My father recalled that he would have given anything at that moment to take just one bite of a potato. Soon he and the others were plotting how to smuggle potatoes back to the hut. The Americans pretended to be working, while they were actually depositing as many potatoes as possible in their pockets. The guards seemed oblivious, or so the Americans thought. "Hunger and greed can drive you to do stupid things," recalled Dad.

It didn't take long for the guards to discover what was up. Suddenly they were coming at the smugglers with gun butts and ordering them to empty their bulging pockets. The POWs were told to lie face down on the frozen ground with their hands over their heads. Clearly, the guards were pissed.

On the ground, Dad was overwhelmed by fear and expecting to be killed. While trying to mentally grasp how serious the situation was, he heard the men next to him quietly whimpering, "Oh God, no." The guards now began to shout at one another. It was typical of them to dis-agree and argue among themselves about how to handle a POW prob-lem. One guard, tired of arguing, began to lightly poke my father and the others with the tip of his bayonet, threatening to kill them. Fortu-nately, their wool coats resisted the sharp point of the bayonet.

In the main yard, Heinz heard the commotion and realized my fa-ther and others he knew were involved. He quickly ran to the aid of his POW friends and tried to diffuse the situation. Heinz informed the guards that the POWs had missed their evening meal the night before because of delays on the train from Munich. He also explained that they also hadn't had any breakfast after being called out of morning roll call. Since Heinz was in charge of the men, he said he would hold them re-sponsible for what had just happened, assigning them extra work for attempting to steal food.

The guards stared blankly at Heinz, unsure of what to do. Finally they relented, handing the Americans over to him. The brilliant Heinz, master of control and deception, knew what buttons to push to get his way. By this point in the war, many of the SS guards were losing their patience with the Third Reich. And they were also overwhelmed by the worsening conditions at the camp. Often it was easier for guards to ig-nore a problem and look the other way, avoiding having to mete out discipline. The potato-stealing escapade was an example of this. Finally it was all over. Holding them at gunpoint, Heinz marched the dirt- and snow-covered prisoners back to their hut without further incident.

Back at the hut "Heinz ripped us all new assholes," my father told my mother. "He was so furious with us he almost couldn't speak. We could have all been killed by the guard for stealing food." My father knew Heinz was right. Greed and stupidity had gotten in the way of clear thinking. Calming down a bit, Heinz told my father's group that the guard who'd gone *verrückt* (crazy) on them had a history of killing POWs. The man was an animal with little patience, Heinz told them, whose best friend was the commandant. He could get away with murder if he liked, Heinz explained, and was known for his ruthless and arrogant behavior. He continued to describe him as a coward who enjoyed killing with the bayonet, because it was quieter and wouldn't draw much attention. According to Heinz, three weeks earlier the man had bayoneted a POW in Munich for throwing a brick. This type of killing, he said, got covered up, often labeled as an accidental death from bombings.

Dad and the others took heed, thanking Heinz for coming to their rescue. He paused before leaving to ask his friends to stay out of trouble, because Christmas was coming. They all promised Heinz, and he left the hut.

THE CHRISTMAS TREE, POW PIE,
AND A CHARCOAL DRAWING

Christmas Eve was just two days away, and now the demeanor of the Nazi guards changed for the better. The Germans were catching the Christmas spirit. It was a big relief for Dad and the other POWs when they learned that the Christmas holidays were important to the Germans. Some semblance of normalcy now replaced the deadliness of prison life. My father and the others in his hut always celebrated Christmas back home, so it was natural to somehow celebrate it here, no matter the conditions. Things were looking up. My dad wrote about this time in his journal:

> On December 23, 1944, we received Red Cross boxes and instructions to share with one other person. It was decided that Bert and I were sharing one box. Normally one box was shared between six men. With this surprise, we had three boxes for the six of us. We now had plenty of food for our Christmas dinner.

My father and his friends decided they deserved a special Christmas celebration, despite the impossible times. They pooled their food to create one big feast. The men in his group were Phil, Bob, Art, Prince, Bert Cottrell, and my father. He called his prison-camp buddies "The Fabulous Six." In his journal Dad mentioned only the first names of the four others in his group, aside from Bert. He mentioned Bert's last name because the two of them had a lot in common. Both came from West Virginia, and both had been captured in France several days apart. Bert and Dad had the privilege of experiencing "hell" together, ending up at Stalag VIIA in the same hut. Bert and my father were extremely close during the war.

Bert was now busy swearing as he ripped the floorboards off the corner of the hut, because he couldn't locate the candles they'd stolen from a bombed-out house in Munich. Bert was the man in charge of storing everything the group acquired in a secret place under the floorboards of the hut. He finally found the candles and began to light them.

On extremely cold days, the men used candles to take the chill out of the air. But now the candles were going to add to the Christmas feeling. Soon all of them were burning, and the men enjoyed a somber moment together. Their side of the hut became very quiet as sadness swept through their hearts.

My father fought back tears of loneliness and abandonment. Each and every POW was thinking of their families and wondering what Christmas back home was going to be like without them. Dad speculated that Eleanore and his family must know by now that he was a prisoner of Nazi Germany. He'd yet to receive any mail from them; thinking about this sent Dad deeper into sadness and despair. He fought back hard against these feelings.

Bert, on the other hand, had a hard time expressing any emotion. During times of reflection, he seemed distant and uninterested. He was a frightened man with no confidence in his future. Bert had been wounded by shrapnel three separate times, in June, July, and August. Amazingly, he'd only taken part in active fighting during those three months. Bert was now entitled to receive three Purple Hearts, one for each wound. Two of his wounds had been superficial, but the third had taken a piece of flesh off the top of his right shoulder. Bert was one lucky man, returning to battle within several days after each of his wounds. To lighten his friend up a bit, Dad often joked that Bert was the only soldier in the entire war who'd been injured every month. "Thank God the Germans captured you, Bert," my dad teased him. "They put a stop to you collecting Purple Hearts monthly."

Bert used his humor and considerable wit to cover up his pain and sadness. Whenever emotions among the men were running high and they began to share stories from home, Bert immediately changed the subject. Dad knew from his long talks with Bert that he honestly believed none of them would ever walk out of the camp alive. He was certain they were all going to die of starvation or be killed in an air raid while on work detail in Munich. No matter how hard Dad tried, he couldn't convince Bert otherwise.

None of the six men in Dad's group had received any mail from home as of December 23, 1944. This only added to poor Bert's pessimism. Unfortunately he'd lost all hope, and his emotions only allowed him to see as far as the barbed-wire fence surrounding Stalag VIIA.

Bert snapped his reflective friends back to reality by announcing, "Tomorrow is Christmas Eve, and we need to get started today if we want to feast on Christmas." Soon everyone was busy with preparations for their holiday meal. Heinz pounded on the door a few hours later and entered the hut. He asked them if they'd like to have a small Christmas tree, explaining that some of the other guards were letting their huts have trees. The commandant was relaxing his standards for Christmas.

Excitement and Christmas energy filled the room. My father recalled for my mother:

Everyone was just amazed that this would even be possible. Now we needed to find stuff to hang on the tree. This was a good thing, because it gave us something to do. Christmas was becoming magical, and all of us caught the Christmas spirit in a big way.

My mother told me that my father's tree looked like it had come from the junkyard. "But they were all very proud of it," she said. "When he told me this story, I thought how ingenious they had all been." My mother explained that their ornaments were pieces of paper, food labels, tufts of dirt, and lint. The nails from the floorboards were also used as decorations. "Your dad's friend Bert unraveled pieces of his wool coat, braiding the threads together to make 'tinsel' to hang on the tree, and tin cans were flattened to be made into ornaments," she said. A cross was placed on the top because they had no way to make an angel. The cross was actually the best choice, the men decided, because clearly they were in need of divine intervention. "Each man prayed hard that the Good Lord would end the war soon, bless them all, and get them out of Stalag," my mother said.

Several hours later, Heinz once again announced his presence by pounding on the hut's door before entering. Heinz was truly a kind and caring individual, even if he wore a Nazi uniform. Seconds before Heinz came inside, my father had finished compiling in his journal the list of food items he'd received in his Red Cross box. He quickly stashed the journal beneath the floorboards, before it could be discovered.

Even given the level of trust and friendship that existed between Heinz and my father, he never let his German friend know that he kept a journal. Dad took copious notes about the items he'd received from the Red Cross. This was his way of remembering what he'd had and when he'd had it. Dad knew that the coming months were going to be hellish, with food becoming ever scarcer in the seriously overcrowded camp. In addition to his food inventory, Dad painstakingly stripped off every label from the cans and boxes and secured them in his journal with the homemade glue he'd made from grinding up crackers into flour, adding a hint of chocolate, and mixing it with water into a thick sticky paste.

———

To this day Dad's journal stands as a visual testament to his Christmas celebration. When I look at the tattered pages and rub my fingers over the labels from the various foods he'd been given, I can sense how important this food from his Red Cross boxes had been to him. Without it he might have died, because he was forced to work and burn calories he didn't have to spare. The Nazis used food as a weapon to gain control over their prisoners. Even after sixty-five years, I can feel his presence in this book and imagine how something as simple as placing food labels in his journal could become so meaningful to him. In the coming months, Dad would look at these pages when he was hungry and think back on that special Christmas Day in 1944, when all of them had plenty to eat and fragments of actual happiness hovered in the air.

Walking around the interior of the hut, Heinz took notice of the Christmas tree and declared that it was the best tree in the entire camp. He also confirmed the truth of rumors that a Christmas celebration was being planned by some of the other American prisoners. For now the commandant was letting this happen. Dad and his friends were elated at this news. Christmas was going to be something special.

———————————

By Christmas Eve everyone on the American side of the camp had been told about the Christmas celebration. Since the American POW population had swelled to around 4,800, the Germans decided to let them use a building that could handle 100 men at one time. The show was scheduled hourly and kicked off its first performance at 8 a.m. My dad and his group attended the third show, at 10 a.m. The opening hymn, "O Come All Ye Faithful," set off so much emotion that many of the soldiers, including my dad, began to cry. Some of the organizers worried they might have to stop the show because emotions were running so strong. But soon both music and laughter could be heard coming from the building. The show was a fantastic mental lift for everyone.

As my father and his friends were leaving the performance, they saw in the distance many Nazis quickly making their way through the snow toward the building. All appeared stern and slightly irritated. Soon a German colonel, several majors, other officers, and about forty junior guards arrived at the door. Fearing the worst, my father and the others expected the Germans to shut down the Christmas show.

Anxiously waiting to see what was going to happen, my father and the others soon heard through the closed door the cheerful sounds of men singing Christmas hymns. My incredulous father could not believe what was happening. The Germans had been seized by the Christmas spirit. For one day, the animosities between the two nations had been forgotten. A rare aura of peacefulness pervaded the camp.

167

Returning to the hut, Dad and his friends were happy men. Now they would put the finishing touches on the feast they all had worked hard to prepare. Even the weather added to the Christmas spirit, with fresh snow covering the ground. An excerpt from my dad's journal:

Today from the three Red Cross parcels I took all the candy and the crackers and ground them to a fine powder and made flour for the pies. Here is how I made the pies for our Christmas Celebration:

One box of Canadian crackers

½ stick of butter (this is all we had)

One tablespoon of salt

Powdered milk, mixed with water to make 1 pint

I mixed all the dry stuff first, then added the milk and mixed until smooth. I added more water until it became the consistency of cake batter. I poured the batter into old tin pans we found in Munich and baked each pie on top of the POW stove. For the filling I took the chocolate and melted it down. I added dry milk and some water, then brought it to a boil, simmered till thick, and poured it into each crust to finish. There you have it, POW pie!

Merry Christmas! December 1944

For the rest of the day the men ate their fill and relaxed, enjoying each other's company. Stories were told and laughter prevailed. Dad had taken Eleanore's tattered picture from his shirt and placed it on the desk to make her a part of the celebration. A POW named Miles found some paper and took cinders of charcoal from the POW stove. As everyone around him talked and laughed, Miles skillfully drew a beautiful portrait of my mother based on the photo on the table.

My father was astonished to discover what Miles had been up to. As he finished the drawing, he looked at my father and said, "This is for you, because your girlfriend is one of the most beautiful women in the world, and I had to draw her." Dad was speechless. This was the best possible prison-camp Christmas gift. Dad carefully displayed the work of art for all the men to see and later placed it inside his journal for safekeeping. Dad carried this portrait inside his journal for the rest of the war. Today my mother's charcoal portrait hangs proudly in my living room.

The evening roll call was canceled. Apparently the Germans were too busy celebrating to pay attention to the American POWs on Christmas Day. Years later, when we celebrated Christmas as a family, I remember Dad reminiscing about how special this day had been to him. According to Dad, he'd had two great days during the war: the day he returned to the shores of America a free man and Christmas Day 1944.

MORALE PLUMMETS AND MAIL ARRIVES

The next day, the Christmas kindness of the German guards had evaporated. It was as if it had never happened. Roll call came at 5 a.m., and works details formed and left the camp. In a few weeks the camp's morale would sink even lower, when rumors began to circulate about extensive fighting by the Allies far to the north. According to the rumors, the Germans had taken thousand of prisoners in that battle.

When my father entered Stalag in late September, the prisoner population was at about 60,289 men. The American population of officers and infantry was hovering at around 1,600 soldiers. As the months progressed, this number would increase dramatically. By January 1945 the American population would grow to 5,767, particularly after the Battle of the Bulge. The Russian prisoners were the largest segment, by far, at slightly over 15,000 men. By February 1945 the entire population was hovering at 76,248 and growing, and conditions were heading for total disaster. Stalag VIIA was now the largest POW camp on the planet. Originally the Germans had designed the camp to hold a maximum of 10,000 persons.

It was early January 1945, and Bert, Phil, and my father were all sitting together when a camp prisoner delivering mail dropped off letters from the U.S. at the table. The men quickly grabbed their respective letters and left the table to seek some privacy.

Dad had a letter. His heart pounding with anticipation, he quickly scanned the return address to see who the letter was from. But he determined it was not from Eleanore or from his parents, as he'd hoped. The broad smile disappeared from his face. Quickly opening it, he saw that the letter was from Elsie Hanna, a close friend of his parents. Many questions arose in his young mind. Why was his first letter at the POW camp from Elsie and not from his parents or Eleanore? If Elsie knew he was a prisoner, surely his parents and Eleanore also knew. Why weren't they writing to him? Baffled and discouraged, he finished reading the letter and placed it between the pages of his journal. He decided not to think about it anymore.

A short time later, revisiting his thoughts, Dad's spirits improved. He was grateful to have received any letter. It dawned on him that Elsie had most likely found out from his parents that he was a prisoner of war. Elsie had written him before his parents got around to it. After all, Dad knew his parents were the type to take their sweet old time before doing anything. Why should this situation be any different? Perhaps more mail would arrive soon.

But the days came and went with no mail from Eleanore or his parents. Now even more troubled, Dad began to ask questions about what was going on with the mail. Heinz reported that some of the men were getting letters from home on a regular basis, many others received them occasionally, and some, like my father, hadn't received any mail at all. There was no way to check or verify the mail. Censoring of mail was also a big problem during the war. If letters contained information not approved by the censors, they would be sent back or destroyed.

Up until his death, my father never really understood the way the mail had worked during the war. But while researching this book, I learned that during the early part of 1945 a large number of letters had been found dumped in the coal pile at Stalag VIIA. While many of them were damaged or destroyed, some eventually made it to the POWs. When they were finally found, the mistake caused a major rift between the Red Cross and the authorities at Stalag VIIA.

Finally, on February 13, 1945, Dad received his first letter from his parents. It was typed and had been started by his mother on December 12, 1944, and finished and mailed five days later. Dad had been spot-on about his parents. His mother had taken her sweet old time writing him a letter. When she finally mailed it, almost two months passed before he received it. Soon after, he began to receive other family letters. My mother wrote my father a letter a day. She was madly in love with him and missed him so much. Unfortunately, he only received a small number of her letters. Some are listed in his journal under the ledger name "Eppie." Dad wrote my mother as often as he could. What troubles me is that none of his letters ever reached her. I am so glad that she never gave up hope for him and married him soon after he returned home. The journal contains only two letters: one from his parents and the letter from Elsie. What happened to the others remains a mystery.

The men were now excited for Bert. Dad and the others thought Bert might gain a new outlook on life after receiving letters from home. They were hoping his spirits would lift, making him feel more positive and less afraid. But sadly this did not turn out to be the case. Bert still held the extreme fear that none of the Fabulous Six would ever make it home from the war. No matter how hard my father and the men tried to convince him otherwise, they couldn't make him into an optimist.

After researching my father's story, I now understand why he insisted that I remain positive, no matter what life's circumstances might throw at me. I was taught to never accept defeat—this was not going to be part of the equation, whatever happened in my life.

War is a ridiculous game that humans play. I am not able to wrap my mind around the meaning of the "rules" of war. How can two countries decide to uphold certain moral and ethical standards by creating rules that must be followed while they are massacring one another? The presence of a neutral party such as the Red Cross does allow for certain

Beer and Belches in Munich

On one trip to Munich, the group was working next door to a German brewery that had been slightly damaged. But its second basement, below the street level, was an intact storage area for wooden barrels filled with beer. Bombs began to fall, and everyone was instructed to take cover in the second basement. Bombs exploded at street level, high above them, and the basement shook and rumbled. Suddenly, a very large barrel let loose, and beer started to pour from its seams. Dad and the others were wild with excitement as the streaming barrel became a fountain of flowing beer. The POWs positioned their mouths strategically, gulping as much beer as possible. The men were taking turns, and with so much beer flowing, the floor was becoming a sea of beer. Even the old German guard was trying to figure out how to partake of this adventure.

Bombs continued to fall, and some of the bricks in the basement ceiling let loose, falling on top of the barrels. No one flinched, no one cared—they all just kept drinking. Another barrel burst open, and everyone turned their attention to it. The bombing finally stopped. Feeling the effects of the beer, the men were now playing belching games. Everyone in the basement began to belch out complete sentences. The men were feeling pretty good, and even the old guard was smiling. Dad remembers laughing so hard his side hurt.

Later that evening, all of them still very drunk, they boarded the cattle cars and were locked in by the guards. As the train headed back to Moosburg, the waste bucket in the corner of the car quickly filled up. Soon they were forced to relieve themselves through the cracks in the walls of the cars. No one cared. The alcohol had dulled their pain and sorrow, and the rocking train soon put them to sleep.

standards to be upheld on both sides. But if you read the rules of war, you can see that they are always broken. We now know that the rules of war were completely ignored in the many Stalag and concentration camps that the Germans created.

During the war the Red Cross monitored all German prison camps that included Allied soldiers. In accordance with the Geneva Conventions, standards of basic care had to be met to protect all captive Allied soldiers. At best, the Red Cross tried doggedly to improve the conditions within each camp. Reports were generated by them and shared with the camp commandants in an effort to improve conditions. In some cases things did improve. Unfortunately, at Stalag VIIA nothing the Red Cross did or suggested in early 1945 could improve this camp. It was a lost cause, sliding downward into a horrific overcrowded slum.

One positive note was America's improving position in Europe. By February 1945, it was clear that American forces were gaining ground and starting to win the war in Europe. As the U.S. Army worked its way toward Germany, it began to draw near other Stalag camps. The Germans hastily evacuated these camps and marched the captured Allied POWs on long death marches during the worst of the winter weather. Many thousands of lives were lost, and the POWs who didn't die suffered from frostbite, disease, and starvation during these brutal marches. Little food was available, and POWs often died in their tracks while marching. Every one of these displaced POWs was headed directly to Stalag VIIA. It explains how the camp became so overcrowded.

In February 2009, I traveled to the National Archives in College Park, Maryland, to research my father's war. While combing the maze of files, I discovered many declassified documents about the conditions at Stalag VIIA that had not been viewed since the war.

In 1945 between February 10 and February 14 the Men of Confidence visited Stalag VIIA. These were neutral parties, selected by the Red Cross, who went into POW camps to identify problems and initiate solutions to them. The report they compiled confirms my father's experiences there. According to the report, American POWs numbered more than 10,000 at the camp. There was insufficient space in most of the barracks for the POWs to lie down. Vermin were everywhere, the buildings were unheated, and many POWs fainted from the lack of air in the overcrowded barracks. No facilities existed for washing dishes or to help maintain bodily cleanliness. A single cold-water spigot served 1,600 men. To make matters even worse, the spigot worked only part of the time. The MOC reported that much of the sickness in the camp was being caused by inedible soup. This report cites my father's barracks as "extremely dirty" and a hazard to health.

HEINZ DISAPPEARS AND DAD PLANS AN ESCAPE

Dad was totally fed up with the conditions within the camp. He was weak and starving all the time. He estimated he'd lost close to forty pounds since his capture. Perhaps worst of all, Heinz had disappeared and had not been seen for more than four days. This was very odd. Dad and the others were becoming increasingly alarmed about his whereabouts. They dismissed their concerns by speculating that he might have been assigned to work in another part of the camp. Of course they couldn't ask anyone about Heinz, because it would jeopardize his life if the other guards realized that he'd befriended his captives.

Dad had made up his mind, informing his group of friends that he was planning an escape within the next several weeks. The planning and timing had to be right, he told them, and most likely he would escape while in Munich on work detail. This news sent the men into shock. They stared at my father as he explained why he needed to escape. The camp conditions were becoming unendurable, he said, and the trips to Munich provided the perfect opportunity. Dad believed they all would be better off leaving and trying to survive on their own, while attempting to reconnect with American troops. The worst thing that could happen to him, he speculated, was that he'd be recaptured and thrown back in prison. He was hoping that Munich would be liberated soon.

By mid-February 1945, Dad was becoming numb to the Munich experience. And he correctly guessed that the Third Reich was unraveling.

It was beginning to dawn on the Nazis and the other Germans that Germany was probably going to lose the war.

In fact, Munich had become a circus that offered a prime opportunity for escape. Stalag was now assigning new guards daily for supervision of work duty. These guards did not know the individual POWs' personalities, and they were old guys, drafted citizens, not of the SS variety, who had wanted nothing to do with the Third Reich before the war. All of the American POWs on work detail were starting to take advantage of this situation by playing stupid, not listening to commands, and acting like children not in the mood to work. They'd just sit down in the rubble whenever they felt like it. Not one guard ever raised his gun to correct this situation. The POWs had become adept at manipulating the system.

My mother, along with POWs or members of their families, verified the following story:

A guard in Munich responsible for my father's work detail fell asleep while on duty. All the POWs noticed and started laughing. A man Dad didn't know had the guts to sneak up behind this sleeping guard, slit his backpack with a knife he'd found in a bombed-out house, and steal all his food. Later that day, when the guard reached for his lunch, he discovered it missing. He was very upset but did nothing about it.

Dad believed he could get away with escaping, because the guards often fell asleep. He could slip away, gaining some distance before anyone noticed he was missing. Dad asked his trusted friends: "Who's in with me on this?" All remained silent.

My father never did anything in his life without a plan. Several months previously, he'd become friends with an elderly German civilian in Munich. Dad had been trading soap and cigarettes for his homemade bread. He spoke perfect English and had lived in the United States for almost fifteen years. Returning to Germany for a visit, he'd been trapped there when the war broke out. Fortunately, he was too old to be drafted into the army, because he hated what Germany had become. His sympathies were with the Americans, and he'd helped others successfully escape months earlier. He was offering his sister's barn with a secret cellar to my father. "I would rather take my chances than die in here of neglect or sickness," Dad told his friends, who were listening intently.

Bert, with uncharacteristic courage, announced that Dad's idea was a good one and volunteered to be his partner. Together they would plan the escape. Dad asked the remaining men one more time: "Who is with me on this other than Bert?" Total silence. For now there would be no more takers for Dad's dangerous idea.

DAD AND BERT ESCAPE

The escape plan was set in stone. It had been several weeks since my father had informed his friends of his intention to escape while on work detail in Munich. Dad had two other "takers" who'd agreed to join him. Everyone expected Bert to back out as the time drew closer, but he was sticking to the plan. Bob, another trusted POW, had also agreed to join the escape.

The three men had all been stockpiling as much soap, cigarettes, and food as they could safely carry without being noticed by the guards. They discussed their plans, feeling pretty confident they could pull off the escape. They believed they were as ready as they would ever be. The risk of being captured in Munich was enormous, so they knew they'd have to get out of town as quickly as possible.

Anticipating the escape, my father's stomach was upset all the time. He was also terribly saddened by Heinz's disappearance. Rumors had been circulating that several guards had been killed because they'd breached security, compromising the camp. The Nazis quickly employed harsh remedies for things of this nature. The rumors were never confirmed. Dad surmised that the Nazis had assigned someone to watch Heinz's every move. Unfortunately, Dad knew that if Heinz had been suspected of treason, the Nazis would have killed him on the spot.

Heinz had exerted a major influence on my father's life as a prisoner of war. They'd become acquainted shortly after my father was captured in Mortain, France, and built their relationship over many months. If not for Heinz's kindness, compassion, and assistance, my dad knew his time as a POW would have been much harder to bear. Shortly after my dad arrived at Stalag, Heinz gave him a picture of himself. Dad pasted it inside his journal, where it is still displayed today.

When I was growing up, I knew about Heinz. Sometimes an event or topic would cause my father to mention him. My mother told me Heinz was one of two men who'd most influenced my father. The other was his father. It was terribly sad for my dad that he would never be able to see his German friend again. My mother told me that many times in their life together my dad mentioned that he had dreamed about Heinz. Dad was certain that he'd been caught red-handed by the SS for aiding and abetting the Americans. Time never healed this wound, even after many decades. Until the moment of his last breath on this earth, my father silently grieved for his German friend.

Shortly before his escape, Dad had decided to leave his journal and the prized relic behind. My father agonized about the fate of his mementoes, but he didn't want to carry them with him. He needed room in his pockets for soap and cigarettes to trade in Munich. My father asked Prince to hold his personal possessions for him. They made a plan to meet after the war, shook hands, and said good-bye.

After the work detail arrived in Munich, Bert, Bob, and Dad were pretty anxious and tense. On this day a friendly old guard was in charge of their group, and the antics of the other POWs were in full force. Like German clockwork, the guard dozed off after lunch. Wasting no time, my father and the others put their plan into motion, slipping quietly away from the rest of the group. With their hearts beating out of their chests, the men negotiated the rubble, the constant strafing of guns, and the American bombs.

Several hours into their escape, the three men were forced to hide among the dead, burying themselves in a pile of mangled bodies and body parts. Silently they prayed they would go unnoticed by the

Germans. The smell of death was awful, but they had to tolerate it to avoid discovery. Within seconds of approaching them, the German soldiers smelled death and quickly left. Soon Dad and his friends were able to move on.

Running, hiding, and deception were the name of the game. Bert, Bob, and Dad were now "wanted" men, and the authorities at Stalag most likely deemed them missing. Their escape was extremely hard on them and nerve-racking. By evening they had arrived, exhausted, in the area where the rendezvous with Dad's German civilian friend was to take place. As planned, the German appeared out of nowhere and motioned to the men to follow him. Arriving at the barn in the dark, the men were placed in the cellar for the night. Given food and water, they were able to relax and converse a bit with the German. "My name is Wolfram," he said, "I know your name, Herbert, but who are your friends?" Dad introduced Bert and Bob. "We all come from the same Stalag hut," he told the German.

Shaking hands all around and thanking Wolfram for his help, the men learned from him that the Allies had recently extended their bombing range. He urged them to be extremely careful. "Shit," said Bob, "I just knew this was going to happen." Now the men were scared and fearing for their lives. They discussed strategy until Wolfram left for his sister's house. Keeping his thoughts close, Dad was now, in fact, very angry. Every damn time we try to make things better in this fucking war, he thought, it is always met with a roadblock. Breaking into Dad's thoughts, Bert and Bob agreed that this escape was far better than the bullshit they had left behind at Stalag. Dad thought they ought to find three dead Germans and steal their uniforms.

After what seemed like hours of discussion, the three decided they'd continue to take their chances in the morning. The witty Bert used humor to soften the reality of the situation: "Where in the hell are we going to go? Let's surrender to the Germans and tell them we're sorry—it was just a big misunderstanding that we escaped from the work detail in Munich." Dad and Bob began to laugh. Dad drifted off to sleep thinking second thoughts, concluding that he should have stayed put at Stalag.

The next morning, after a good night's rest, the three men had recovered their confidence. They vowed to remain together and travel to more remote areas in Bavaria, where the scarcity of German soldiers meant a real chance for freedom. The hope that the war would be ending soon was a plausible theory. But they knew that American soldiers were making good progress through Europe, heading to the heart of Nazi Germany. Wolfram briefed Dad, trying to reassure him that if they made it to the mountains, they'd have a good chance of finding shelter with sympathetic German farmers. It was a risky adventure but worth a try.

Suddenly bombs were falling all around, strafing the outskirts of Munich with full force. The ground shook as pieces of the barn structure began to fall on them. Surrounded by dust and debris, Bert and Wolfram began to panic. Wolfram ordered them to leave the cellar immediately, fearing that the barn might collapse.

Grabbing what they could, they scrambled up the wooden stairs to the ground floor and buried themselves in hay. Wolfram wished them luck, before returning to his house and his sister. The bombs rained down, scaring them out of their wits. Dad was reminded of Operation Cobra. His heart racing from panic and fear, Dad called out to his friends, "Let's get the hell out of here." The three POWs ran from the barn into a nearby field. "Holy shit," shouted Dad, as the bombs kept falling.

Bert and Bob spotted a destroyed house in the next field over, and the three men took off at a full run. The bombing stopped as they arrived at the house. The quiet was deafening, although their ears continued to ring. Silence was broken by the familiar sounds of a German soldier barking orders: *"Bewegen Sie sich nicht"* ("Halt").

CAPTURED

How the hell could this be happening to me again? thought my father. Soon, more than four German guards were aiming their rifles at the men. None of the Germans spoke any English. Somehow they instantly understood that Dad, Bert, and Bob had escaped from Stalag VIIA. One of the guards said, as he gestured with his gun, *"Stammlager, Stammlager, Moosburg, yea?"* The prisoners nodded their heads. Then the Germans started laughing, saying *"Dumme Amerikaner."*

The Germans were not particularly hostile. Gesturing for the men to start walking in the direction of Munich, they didn't even bother to search them. It was a bittersweet moment for Dad, who was relieved to have survived the bombing and avoided being shot by the Germans. They could have been executed on the spot. "Thank you, God," prayed Dad silently as he walked. But the low point of the bittersweet moment was their imminent return to the horrific conditions inside Stalag VIIA. Understandably worried, Dad, Bert, and Bob knew they were heading for solitary confinement.

Bert quietly said, "We've lost our beds and sleeping areas and are now the newcomers to the camp." He was, of course, right. The walk back to Stalag VIIA was slow and arduous. The guards strolled along, laughing and telling stories. Dad and his friends picked up only a few of the words, but it was clear these guys didn't have a care in the world.

Eventually they arrived back at the work area in Munich and reunited with the POWs. The soldiers who'd captured them explained to the Munich guards what had happened. Dad, Bert, and Bob were isolated inside a boxcar for several hours before it was time to head back to the prison camp.

The train arrived at the station late. Dad, Bert, and Bob were immediately taken to the solitary confinement area of the camp. Not a single German spoke to them, and they didn't meet with the commandant. Justice was served up quickly, without a trial or any discussion of why they'd decided to escape. Dad and his friends now had their chance to endure the horrors of no food and almost no water. The first night was a cold one, and they slept on the floor without any covers, huddling together for warmth. They were miserable, but thankful to be alive.

Dad did most of his heavy thinking before falling asleep. He understood just how bad it was likely to be in here. He remembered tossing morsels of bread over the fence to help out the starving and depressed guys in solitary confinement. Now he was going to be part of this misery, and he wondered how long it would last. Driving the ominous thoughts from his mind, he let sleep take over.

The next morning Dad was stiff and sore when he picked himself up off the floor. Boredom and starvation were about to become his major problems. Dad found water, but breakfast was not going to be an option. At roll call he and his friends were astonished to see the size of the population in solitary confinement. The guards read their names from the ledgers—the efficient Germans had already processed their paperwork.

Dad and his friends did not eat for five days. As expected, they were allowed just enough water to keep them alive, and the floor continued to be their beds. Delirious from fatigue and extreme hunger, they were sick and rapidly losing weight. To conserve energy, Bert and Bob stopped talking. Dad obsessed about someone tossing a morsel of food over the fence. He fixated on this fantasy almost every moment. Solitary confinement was topping all of his previous experiences at being nearly starved to death.

The physical effort and emotion they'd expended on the attempted escape also took a toll on the men. On the evening of the fifth day, the three of them were placed back in the main camp in a hut next to the one where they had previously lived. The overcrowding in solitary confinement had led to their premature release. The Nazis were running out of room.

Bert, Bob, and my father immediately went to see their old friends. A shocked Prince, Art, and Phil could not believe their eyes. After greetings and handshakes, the former escapees went to dinner. Food made them feel slightly better, and they began to tell the story of their escape and unfortunate recapture. Prince said he hadn't been expecting to return my father's journal and relic so soon. My father smiled as he took them back. "I had deep regrets about leaving them," he said. "I'll never do that again. In the future, I'm not going anywhere without these." My father surprised Prince with his comments. Did he mean that he was going to try to escape again? "Yes, I'm getting out of here," Dad said. The Fabulous Six were in total shock and disbelief. After the trauma the three men had endured, how could Herbert even think of doing it all again? Dad answered decisively, explaining that he was now more determined than ever to get out of Stalag. Everyone dropped the subject. Perhaps Herbert was just angry or still a little delusional from his ordeal. They decided to call it a night and went to sleep.

Several weeks passed before the subject of escaping came up again. Dad was still thinking about Heinz every day and couldn't stop wondering what had happened to his friend. Every day more prisoners entered the camp, coming from far away with stories to tell of the substantial progress American forces were making in Europe. It seemed it would not be long before the war was over. March passed and quickly turned into early April. Spring and a new confidence overtook my father—he became more determined than ever to get out of Stalag.

An American prisoner who'd just entered the camp talked of a horrible concentration camp just west of Munich called Dachau. In this camp, Russian prisoners who'd been transferred from Stalag VIIA were being gassed to death or shot against a firing wall. Jews, homosexuals, or anybody who was not considered a perfect enough human being by the Nazis were being executed. If you got close to the camp, the American told them, you could see the thick black smoke rising up from the crematoriums that the Nazis used to cover up the evidence. Dad and the others were horrified and deeply angry at what they had just heard. They understood that the Nazis would take any steps necessary to make the Third Reich dominant across Europe.

Werner Schwartz, a Stalag VIIA historian and former resident of Moosburg, told me the following in 2009:

> The Third Reich was loaded with hate. The British and Americans were held responsible for air raids and were confronted with hatred, especially on work duty in Munich. Italians, formerly German allies, were treated as traitors. The French were treated the best by the Nazis. The Russians were the worst-off group because, according to Nazi ideology, they were subhuman. The Russians didn't receive any Red Cross parcels, and their political commissars were murdered in Dachau, which was very close to Moosburg.

When I was growing up, I observed that my father could be very stubborn. If he made a decision, no one on this planet except my mother could influence him to change it. Amazingly, my mother was able to sway him to her side almost every time. My mother told me that his stubbornness stemmed from his captivity. Others perceived Dad's extreme stubbornness as insensitive and uncaring. But they didn't know anything about the pain he'd endured or the incredible will he'd had to summon up in order to survive.

THE SECOND ESCAPE

In early April my father's stubbornness hit an all-time high when he decided to escape once again from Stalag VIIA. Now the camp was so overloaded with prisoners that Dad was sure he'd be better off living in the woods than inside the camp. Hope for eventual liberation combined with dread and uncertainty. Everyone, including the guards, was miserable and starving. The guards were quickly losing faith in Nazi Germany, and the senior guards knew that the place was unraveling at the seams.

My dad's line of reasoning went something like this: Conditions in all of Germany, and especially in the German Army, were rapidly eroding into pandemonium, chaos, and uncertainty. American forces were drawing closer, and this was his opportunity to reunite with them. Even if he was captured again and returned to Stalag VIIA, he wouldn't be any worse off than he already was. The guards were under stress and tired of responding to POW "incidents." My dad's motto was: "Better to try, than to not try at all." He started making plans.

This war was eroding everyone's spirits. Dad brought up his next escape in conversations with his buddies, announcing that he would be leaving soon. Dad's friends were silent, and sadness filled their hearts. They tried to discourage him, and he came to understand that no one would be joining him. He began to ask some of his other friends in the camp and was amazed to learn that several others were planning to escape as well. He found six men who shared his views and wanted desperately to get out of the camp. Three of them, including my father, had previously tried to escape. Dad believed their collective experience was going to be an asset.

Something in my dad was eating him alive. He knew he had to do this. Dad asked one more time if any of the Fabulous Six would consider joining him. He received the answer he'd expected: no one else had the courage. Bert tried in vain to convince my father to stay and wait for liberation.

Finally the day came, and the determined escapees climbed on the boxcars to be taken to Munich. Dad said tearful goodbyes to all of his buddies, wishing them well. Dad's journal lists the names and the addresses of many of his POW buddies, and, of course, the names of the Fabulous Six are all there. This time Dad took his journal and the relic with him. Bert had helped him make a pocket inside his coat for his mementoes. They took some excelsior from a POW mattress and carefully wrapped up the items.

Bert was very sad. His buddy from West Virginia was leaving him. They had been through so much together in the last eight months. Holding back the tears, they said goodbye and tried to be strong. Dad began to mingle with the men at the farthest corners of the work detail, away from the guards. He was slowly slipping away from sight. Turning back to glance one more time at his friend, my father grinned and waved goodbye. Bert was in distress, unsure if his decision to stay had been the right one. Reacting instinctively, Bert changed his mind and tried frantically to catch my father's eye before he disappeared from view. Bert couldn't shout or run, because it would draw the attention of the guards. He began to wildly wave his hand, trying to make my father understand that he had changed his mind. Feeling desperate, he began to mouth the words, "I'm coming, I'm coming."

Dad was about to turn away for the last time, when out of the corner of his eye he saw Bert's waving hand. He figured Bert was just messing around, as he typically did at times like this. But he began to understand the words Bert was silently mouthing. Now smiles filled their faces. They moved closer together, and Dad pretended to be picking up some debris. Bert finally reaching my father and told him, "I'm coming with you."

Now both of them started moving as far away as possible from the group, finally slipping from view. Bert whispered to my father, "I just had to come. You are right, Stalag is a pit." A short time later, all the escaping men met up and started making their way to the south of Munich. Their destination was the mountains of Austria. They were hoping to run directly into American forces. Dad and the others had no idea where the German or American forces were. They had made up their route based on information obtained from the other camp prisoners who'd been arriving daily.

The massive pile of rubble that had once been the vibrant city of Munich was beginning to vanish behind them, to be replaced by fields, forests, and streams and the aroma of pine trees and country air. They were in a clearing in the woods when they heard the sounds of familiar plane engines approaching. They knew they were hearing American forces heading back to Munich or to other places in Germany. Dad, Bert, and the others ran out from cover to announce their presence. The American pilots could see the POWs waving at them in the clearing and dipped their wings to acknowledge their presence. Several of the planes doubled back to repeat their greeting. The planes couldn't land or even radio American ground forces to report the position of the POWs. Rescue wasn't a possibility.

The men continued their odyssey, slowly making their way into the countryside. It had been nearly six hours since their escape from the Stalag work detail in Munich. They were carefully avoiding Germans, both soldiers and private citizens.

Dad paused for a moment, closing his eyes to take a deep breath of spring air. He hoped it would help clear his mind and settle his emotions. Dad's reverie took him back to a much happier time as a child in West Virginia. The spring countryside seemed very familiar. He visualized the terrace hill where he had lived as a boy loaded with spring flowers. Of course, he knew that as soon as he opened his eyes the nightmare of the war would be staring him in the face again. There was no way to escape it.

Bert, on the other hand, was edgy and fearful they'd all be captured again soon. Extremely paranoid, he was like a cat on the prowl constantly looking for trouble. Bert's uneasy feelings were now spreading to the other men. It wasn't long before all seven of them were jumpy and more nervous than ever. Freedom came with an emotional cost. The longer they were free, the faster their emotional health declined. Dad's good spirits had vanished. Their existence as free men was tainted by physical exhaustion and existential fear.

———

Dad was beginning to lose it mentally. Flashbacks from previous horrific events were running uncontrolled through his mind, and he understood that he was in danger of being shot or captured. Determined to muster the emotional strength to press on, he vowed to never let this happen.

From the moment of his capture by the Nazis back in August, Dad had been experiencing feelings of loss and abandonment. He was, in particular, suffering from the loss of his freedom. Dad had lost his innocence as well. He'd witnessed the brutal treatment of helpless men by Nazi guards. And he'd learned that if a soldier's culture and beliefs were not in line with the Third Reich, he was destined for mistreatment or death. Being a POW gave him a bird's eye view of the worst the Nazis had to offer. But, still, he knew he was lucky that he was an American and not a Russian.

A moonless sky meant that continuing on that night would be impossible. Using a flashlight or fire stick to guide them was out of the question, because it would only alert the Germans to their presence. The men made it safely to a small barn that had been partially destroyed. Emotions were running low. They believed they were marked men and likely to be captured again soon. The entire area was teeming with Nazi soldiers or Nazi sympathizers. As the men discussed their options, the confidence they'd displayed earlier was long gone.

Remarkably, they hadn't yet formally introduced themselves to one another. Dad knew only Bert and the British soldier, Stephen, who had masterminded this escape attempt. Bursting with spit and vinegar, he was a seasoned infantryman and a natural-born leader. Stephen had escaped one other time and been recaptured. Like my father, he wanted out no matter what. Stephen was different from the other POWs in that he'd been at Stalag VIIA for almost two years, and he was very vocal in his hatred of Nazi Germany. The introductions in the barn revealed a mix of nationalities: two British, three Americans, and two Russians made up the group. When the Russians introduced themselves, the five other escapees immediately focused all of their attention on them.

The Russians spoke broken English, but you could still understand what they were saying. The only thing my father couldn't understand was how to pronounce and write their names. In his journal Dad referred to the men as "Russian POWs." As they told their stories of hate and brutality, it became clear that they were marked for death. The Nazis hated Russians, believing them to be traitors against the Third Reich and lower than scum. It was a only a matter of time before they faced starvation, severe abuse, or death.

The two Russian men were from Dachau, the concentration camp near Munich. Most of its prisoners were Jewish and Russian people. A true Nazi extermination camp, Dachau was a terrifying place that participated in medical experiments and torture and used poisonous gas to eliminate the races deemed inferior by Nazi Germany. The constant prisoner cremations were causing the putrid stench and thick black smoke that rose from the camp each day. The shattered city of Munich had become a melting pot for POW work details, including some of the prisoners from Dachau. All of the Stalag and concentration camp POWs near Munich converged in the city center to clean up the massive piles of rubble from American bombs.

That morning the two Russian POWs had been forced to go to Munich for work detail. My father's group was nearby, and when they saw Stephen making a move, they cannily deduced what he was up to and followed him. They'd decided that anything was better than waiting to die. Normally Russians did not intermix with other nationalities on work detail, but the crumbling Nazi infrastructure was compromising all the rules. That night in the barn, when Bert and Dad heard about the Russian prisoners' experiences, they understood more than ever that the horrors of life as an American POW were inconsequential in comparison to the horrors of life as a Russian POW.

Dad's feelings of solidarity with his new Russian friends gave him a nice emotional lift. The men shared what food they had between them, and soon all was quiet as they bedded down for the night. They had organized a night shift, planning to have one person on watch throughout the night.

First light was breaking and Dad couldn't sleep anymore. He took over the watch from one of the Russians, who immediately fell asleep. Dad remembered he had a small pencil tucked away in one of his pockets. Taking his war journal from the back of his pants, he turned to a blank page and began to draw a scene from memory. The sketch is on page eighty-three of his journal, and it depicts his special group of friends gathered around the POW stove. My mother made certain that I clearly understood that my father had drawn this scene early in the morning of the second day of his second escape. Dad finished the drawing and began to stare off into space, wondering what would eventually happen to everyone in the barn. They had no way of knowing what was actually going on in the war, although rumors were rife that the Allies were making progress and getting closer.

Stephen had informed the others the night before that the conditions on his side of Stalag VIIA had deteriorated to an all-time low. Many of the men were very sick, and he predicted that if something was not done soon, the entire camp would be overrun with dysentery and disease. Prisoners were now dying at an alarming rate, and Dad was glad he was no longer there. But, mulling over his situation, he wondered just where he should be right now. At that moment hell looked the same to him whether he was starving and rotting away in a prison camp or sitting in an old barn trying to run away from the Nazis. All Dad could do was pray. He prayed that their ordeal would come to a happy ending soon. He prayed hard for Bert, who Dad knew was going to need an added dose of confidence to carry on. It was obvious to my father that Bert found comfort and solace in spending time with him.

Soon the others began to wake up to bright sunshine filtering in through the holes in the barn. It was cold outside, with frost still present in low-lying areas. The warmth of the spring sun after a good night of sleep helped to reignite some positive spirit in each of them. and they hoped that this day might be a little more tolerable than the one before. Little did they know what was actually in store for them in the hours to come. Two men would not survive, and those who did were in for a new level of trauma that would scar their personalities for the rest of their lives.

CAPTURED AGAIN

During the forty-eight years of their life together, my father spoke to my mother often and in great detail about his second escape from Stalag VIIA.

The sun was now peeking over the hills and shining brightly. Dad turned his back to catch the warmth of its rays. It felt good and was a nice relief from the cold, damp conditions of the day and night before. They shared the small amount of food they had left between them, about enough to fill the palm of each man's hand. Bert found a stream and collected some water in an old rusty bucket that had a hole in the side from a lone bullet. Sticking his finger in the hole, he dipped it into the stream and filled it with ice-cold mountain water. The men washed down their dry bread with a gulp of cold water, bringing back the chill they'd worked so hard to get rid of.

Soon they were ready to move out. Dad was great at navigation and always knew which way he was going no matter what the time of day. The men quickly picked up on his keen navigation skills, relying on him to provide direction. As they discussed the day's strategy, each man instinctively knew their days of freedom were numbered. It would be a miracle if they ran into the Allies and were liberated. Yesterday's run-in with the American planes had made it crystal clear that American forces were not in the area to rescue anyone. The ground forces were likely a long way off, and now the men were outlaws on the run with no place to go. Dad was regretting his decision to escape, and he guessed that the others were thinking the same thoughts. Anxiety hovered in the air between them as they silently continued on to nowhere.

⸻

Meanwhile, a small group of German soldiers were on the prowl in the countryside around Munich. Arriving at the barn where the POWs had spent the night, they went inside to take a look around. They quickly figured out that people had recently been there. A Nazi soldier skilled at tracking put his hand into the hay where the POWs had slept and felt its warmth. He found a bar of Red Cross soap nestled in the hay and held it up to the other Nazis, saying, *"Sie waren hier"* (they were here). The hunt for the POWs was on.

Dad and his group were less than a mile away from the barn and the Germans. Zigzagging across the terrain to stay undercover, the POWs hadn't made much progress. The Nazis scanned the field with binoculars and before long spotted the POWs running between the trees. Entering a thick forest, they decided to stop and eat the rest of their rations. Soon they headed off through the forest again, eventually coming to an abandoned farm. The men lay in wait at the edge of the field, making sure no one was around. Finally they began to slowly work their way to the edge of the barn and then into the house. The previous occupants had clearly left in a hurry. Bert and some of the others were looking everywhere for food. They went down to the cellar, while the rest of the men stood guard.

"Bingo!" called Bert. Deep in the corner of the cellar he'd found apples, potatoes, and nuts. The excited men let down their defenses and went to investigate. Dividing up the food, they carried their individual treasures upstairs. Soon everyone was busy eating and struggling with pulling every morsel of nut out of the shells. The nuts were the best find, providing the nourishment and calories they needed to continue their journey. The apples and potatoes were surprisingly good. Their joy was short-lived. "When you are starving and you suddenly have food available," Dad recalled, "everything gets put on hold until your belly is full."

This occasion was no different. They'd forgotten to assign someone to stand watch.

The Nazis tracking the men had quietly made their way to the farm and surrounded the house. My father told my mother, "Knowing we were distracted by our food, the Nazis decided they had time for a quick cigarette as they waited patiently for us to exit the house." Their bellies full, the men left the house, walking straight into the arms of the Germans, who were ready with their guns aimed. *"Glücklich jetzt? "* (Happy now?) asked the head guard.

Dad was a little relieved that his ordeal was over. The stress of being a fugitive was beginning to take its toll. Bert was just short of petrified. The Nazi guards numbered ten and they clearly meant business. The lead guard spoke almost perfect English. "Where did you think you all could go?" he asked. "Nobody escapes from a Nazi prison camp—not even you. We discovered the place where you were sleeping last night. Do any of you recognize this?" He held up the bar of Red Cross soap. "Stupid Americans," said the Nazi.

A spirited discussion broke out among the Germans. They kept glancing at the POWs. Finally one of the Nazi guards asked to see each man's dog tags. The American and British POWs took off their tags and handed them to the guard. The two Russian POWs didn't have any tags to give to the Germans and this prompted a series of questions. With no responses coming from the Russian men, the guard pressed his questions harder. One of the Russians finally explained to the Nazi in Russian that they were not American, British, or French. Of course the guards knew that they'd captured the two missing Russian POWs. The others could tell that the tone of the conversation had taken a bad turn. The guards divided the captured POWs into two groups. The Russians were placed on the left and rest of the men on the right. Dad's group was being guarded by seven Nazis who ordered them to start marching away from the Russian prisoners.

Nothing more was said. Dad was amazed that he and the others hadn't been searched for weapons. He could tell they weren't going back to Stalag VIIA by the direction they were headed. The camp was to the northwest and they were heading south. This caused my father some concern. Looking back, he could see that the Russians were being taken to the west toward a thick forest.

The peppery Stephen was not afraid to ask questions. "Where are the Russians being taken?" he asked bluntly. The Nazis ignored him. About ninety minutes after they'd been separated from the Russians, they arrived at a large river. The guards ordered everyone to take a drink of water from the stream and then rest. Bert and Dad still had some nuts left to eat, and they asked the guards if they could share them with the group. They were given permission and soon the men were intently concentrating on opening the nuts. The guards seemed uninterested and bored.

Sitting in the warmth of the afternoon sun, Bert, Stephen, and Dad were trying to figure out where they were heading. They could tell that something was not quite right. Dad mentioned to his friends that Stalag was in the other direction from where they were heading. Hearing this, Bert began to panic. Dad told him to calm down and focus on survival, which he was eventually able to do. As the time passed, anxiety and fear were once again seizing hold of the men. Even Stephen's demeanor had changed. It was obvious to my father that this peppery British soldier was now very concerned for his future.

My mother told me that Dad's group waited about an hour before moving out. Throughout this time the guards remained silent. The POWs were feeling very uncomfortable. Suddenly, two gunshots rang out from the distant and quiet wilderness, echoing through the hills and startling the men. One of the guards turned his gaze to the POWs. Breaking his silence, he said in English, "Your Russian friends are now dead."

The faces of the five POWs displayed shock and dismay. Was this to be their fate as well? Dad, Stephen, and Bert fought back tears. The Nazi guards were impenetrable and even slightly amused by their pain and anguish. "Get up, we are moving out," shouted one of the guards. "You can never trust a Russian." As Dad walked, memories from the last year flooded his mind. He theorized that these Nazis had no intention of killing British or American escapees. It would look far better for them to bring their prisoners in alive. He settled on this scenario, refusing to let his mind wander to any other possibilities. As Dad walked along, he placed his hand on the relic in his pocket and prayed for some kind of divine intervention.

Soon one of the Nazi guards began to speak in English, announcing that the Germans were winning the war against America. He said that earlier in the month President Franklin Roosevelt had committed suicide because he realized he was not going to defeat the German Army. This so-called "news" sent Dad and the others into total shock. Could this be true, they wondered, or was it just Nazi propaganda? With every step, Dad could see the fear increasing in the eyes of his buddies. The emotions of the five men were in shambles. They didn't know what to believe, where they were going, or if they would ultimately survive.

Dad was so overwhelmed that he actually began to wonder if he would be better off dead. But, according to my mother, my father fought hard to improve his mental attitude. He managed to regain some of his fiery spirit, accepting his situation and planning how he might improve it.

Soon they met up with another group of German soldiers. Overhearing the conversations between the Nazis, the POWs understood that they were heading to Austria to somewhere near Salzburg. Eventually one of the guards who spoke English told the men that they would not be returning to Stalag VIIA. He explained that they were being transferred to Stalag XVIIIC, which was south of Salzburg, Austria. Breaking the silence, Stephen spoke up and asked the German why they were being taken there. The soldier glared at Stephen and changed the subject, saying they'd be traveling by train to the next camp. But the persistent Englishman fired off another question: "I'm assuming you are taking us away from our original camp because of the overcrowding and disease or because the American forces are closing in on Stalag VIIA and are about to liberate it. So, which is it?"

Dad was shocked by Stephen's question and so was the German guard, who was now very pissed at all of them. "Silence," he shouted.

He was in a rage and began to ramble on about how the Americans "haven't seen anything yet." Stephen was amused and cracked a slight smile, realizing he'd succeeded at irritating the German. Soon the men were left alone to converse quietly among themselves. Dad told my mom that the German's anger cheered them up considerably. They guessed he was reacting defensively to the suggestion that the Allies were closing in on Moosburg and Stalag VIIA. A true-blue Nazi wasn't about to admit that the Germans were losing the war.

———

They arrived at a train depot in a small town where they were loaded into boxcars. Dad and his group were put in a boxcar in the middle of the train, which calmed them down considerably. They knew they were less likely to take a direct hit from American bombs. "We were put on the boxcars, and they were jammed to the roof with men," my dad told my mother. "We were each given a quart of water but no rations. For four days we were locked in this boxcar traveling to lower Austria."

Inside the boxcar Dad encountered a mix of nationalities that included many POWs from Stalag VIIA. It was evident to the men that the Nazis were moving POWs from northern camps to the south, away from the approaching American forces. The rumors were flying inside. Once the doors were slammed shut and locked, the evening light disappeared and the men were in total darkness.

Dad whispered to Bert in the darkness, "Are you OK?" Bert answered him, and before long individual conversations in the boxcar had converged into one big discussion. Already Dad was hearing from the men who had been sent out of Stalag VIIA that conditions had worsened in the last several days. In a transcript of an interview my father had with the Veterans Administration in 1986, he spoke about his imprisonment:

Just before we escaped for the second time from Stalag VIIA, typhus broke out inside the camp. Now I've never told this to anybody else—this is the first time I have ever brought this incident up—but men were dying like flies. They weren't even burying them. Once they were dead, they were taken from the camp and piling up the bodies like cordwood. Everywhere you looked you could see piles of bodies from men who died of typhus."

Soon the train jerked and started to squeal as it moved away from the station. Their speed increased and the wheels ringing on the rails made conversation almost impossible. Now all was quiet inside the train as some of the men, piled up against one another, drifted off to sleep. The putrid smell of human waste hung in the air—the bucket in the corner hadn't been emptied in several days. Occasionally a breath of fresh air would work its way into the boxcar through the many holes and cracks, offering the men the smell of freedom. As the train rocked down the tracks, the men captive inside were unaware of what was going to happen to them next.

About an hour into the ride the train suddenly ground to a halt. Most of the men were now awake, wondering what was happening. The wafts of fresh air were a thing of the past. Body heat was building inside the boxcar, making the temperature very uncomfortable. One hour turned into three and three hours became twelve. When their sojourn in the boxcar was finally over, my father and the others had endured four days, with just one quart of water for each man. When I asked my mom how they'd survived with the spring sun beating down on the boxcar, she replied, "I asked him the same thing. He told me it was fortunate they'd had cloudy days with lots of rain. He said, 'Once we got used to all the body heat it was pretty comfortable inside, but everything else was just miserable.' "

There was not much to do except sleep, talk, and conserve water. Nobody inside that train had any idea how long they would be stranded on the tracks. Some of the men grew angry, some cried, and some, like my father and Stephen, continued to smolder with rage.

On the second night in the boxcar, the train was hit by an air raid. When my father and the others had peeked through the cracks, they'd noticed they were parked adjacent to trains that were hauling oil. These cars were strung together and ready to be transported to wherever the

Germans needed them. The men were sure hoping they were marked as a POW train, but they had no idea. Late that night P-38s began to scream overhead, waking the men up. The sounds of bombs exploding nearby sent cold shivers through all of them. They could hear thunderous explosions as the bombs ignited the oil in the boxcars. Soon the dark night had taken on a warm orange glow, and panic in the boxcar was widespread. Some of the men, including my father, shit in their pants from the extreme stress.

But, pretty quickly, there was nothing left to bomb. Some of the men inside Dad's boxcar began to laugh nervously as they realized they'd been spared. A cheer went up. The chaos receded, and all that was left was the soft afterglow of burning oil. Dad mentioned to mom years later that it had been like a big bonfire. The colors of the flames reminded him of other days in the past year.

At dawn the men were finally moved. Amazingly, the tracks in front of Dad's train were intact. The skill of American P-38 bomber pilots had once again been demonstrated. With a sudden jerk the train was under way. They traveled for about six more hours before making their final stop. The doors opened, and the men were instructed to get out and line up in a single row alongside the train. They were all stiff and sore and smelled so bad that even the flies were avoiding them. Dad remembered squinting his eyes for a very long time as he tried to adjust to the bright daylight.

Dad, Bert, and Stephen stood together wondering what might be coming next. As the Germans barked out orders, each man was given bread and a cup of soup. The men inhaled the food and started looking for more. It was announced that they would be transported to the camp, where they could expect hot showers and more food. Dad recalled that none of the POWs showed any emotion. All of them were tired of a war that was slowly killing them through starvation, emotional abuse, and extreme cruelty. The men climbed onto trucks for the ride to the POW camp, arriving after several hours in the small Austrian mountain town of Markt Pongau. It was close to Stalag XVIIIC, where my father would spend the final month of the war.

A SECOND STALAG AND THE HOLE

My father arrived outside of Stalag XVIIIC on April 16, 1945. At first all seemed uneventful. The camp appeared more or less like any other crappy Nazi prison camp, although this one was a true concentration camp that exterminated Jewish and Russian prisoners. The men immediately noticed that it wasn't overcrowded like Stalag VIIA.

Looking over the maze of German guards, Dad identified some of the same men who'd captured him outside of Munich only days before. My father was now beginning to worry. He expected to pay dearly for his attempted escape, but for now nothing seemed out of the norm.

Several of the guards rounded up the men who'd been on the train and separated them into groups. Bert, Stephen, and Dad, along with six others, were kept outside the camp, away from the other POWs.

The guards began to interrogate Dad and the others. When his turn came, he faced endless questions about his adventures. Dad was willing to give them more information than he had on previous occasions, because nothing he said would betray the U. S. Army and its war strategies. He'd been a prisoner of war for eight months and was hoping that the Germans' questions might lead to some clues about what was really happening in the war. What the guards wanted to find out from him was centered on his Stalag VIIA camp and work experiences. Dad was puzzled about why his Nazi interrogator was so consumed with life at Stalag VIIA and the Munich work details.

Suddenly the conversation turned sour. Dad and the others understood they were in trouble. The guards ordered them to head into the woods far away from the camp; the men suspected they were walking into hell. Finally the Nazis ordered them to stop. My father, first in line, was told to walk to the edge of a large hole in the ground.

Standing solitary confinement was the punishment he and the others were about to endure. My father suffered terribly during this ordeal. Standing in place for so many hours resulted in leg-circulation problems that plagued him for the rest of his life. This cruel confinement, coming after everything else he had experienced in the war, was a blunt blow to my dad's mental health.

His heart beating frantically and suffused with raw panic, Dad expected to be shot. But as he looked into the hole, he realized it wasn't one of the Nazis' signature mass graves. Around him he saw similar holes. The guards hastily retrieved ropes from their packs, placing them securely around my father's waist. One of the nastier guards, speaking in perfect English, ordered my dad to grab the rope and start climbing down into the hole. Dad did what he was told, believing that if he resisted or talked back he would be killed. He reached the bottom of the hole, and the Nazis instructed him to release the ropes so they could pull them back up. Standing alone in the damp and cramped hole, Dad understood that this was going to be the punishment for his second escape.

The hole was deep, and, even with my father's 6' 2" height and his arms fully extended, there was no way he could reach the top to pull himself out. Once all the POWs were situated in their holes, the Nazi guards abandoned them. The loneliness and despair, combined with the overwhelming claustrophobia of feeling as if he had been buried alive, was almost more than my father could bear. "It was so horrible and frightening that I wanted to die," he told my mother. "I was extremely scared and angry the entire time. I even cursed the army for placing me in this situation in the first place," he said. "After it was certain the guards had left the area, I tried yelling to Bert and Stephen, but there was no way any of them could hear my voice. I could hear the distant sound of muffled voices and took satisfaction in knowing that my friends were still alive and kicking."

All my father could see around him were dirt walls. He worried that they might cave in, but the walls were rock hard and he couldn't even dig into them with his hands. The holes had been sized to administer the perfect standing torture. It would take an act of God or men with ropes to remove him from this nightmare. My dad's only option was to muster up the guts and will to survive. Above he could see the trees and sky. Reaching for the relic deep in his pocket, he wrapped his fingers around it and began to pray.

Darkness fell and the situation became more intense. The sky was cloudy, and the night so dark that Dad couldn't see his hand when he placed it directly in front of his face. He understood that his destiny was beyond his control. All he could do was think, stand, and try to stabilize the fear that overwhelmed him. The Nazis were in charge.

Fortunately it didn't rain that night, and the temperature was mild. As the hours passed my father began to disengage mentally. Escalating pain in his lower back and legs was becoming unbearable. My mother said that at one point my father pulled out his war journal, placing it under his shoes in an effort to cushion himself from the hard ground. This worked briefly but soon he returned the journal to his pants, using it to cushion his back as he leaned against the hard dirt wall.

At the first light of dawn my father sensed someone in the area. He vaguely remembered hearing commotion in the night. Later he learned that the disturbance he'd heard had come from guards returning to the holes to check on the men. They'd discovered Bert unconscious, slumped over, and suffering from severe dysentery. The guards removed him from the hole and took him back to the camp. Dad did not remember the last hours of his confinement, nor did he remember being removed from the hole. The Nazis had successfully broken his spirit, reducing his confidence to zero.

My mother was crying when she told me about Dad's return to the camp. He was exhausted and broken, she said. Unable to walk, he'd been carried from the hole. Rebelliousness and a stubborn determination to survive had saved him.

When Dad was removed from the hole, he was taken to the camp by the guards who'd captured him outside Munich. Revenge and hate dominated the minds of these men, and meting out harsh punishment to the American POWs for their failed escape attempt presented no moral problem for them. After all, they'd had no problem killing the two Russian POWs in cold blood just for being Russian. And it hadn't troubled the guards to keep the POWs locked in a boxcar parked outside the fuel depot for four days with very little water and no food while American bombs rained down around them.

To his dying day my father agonized over two scenarios he constructed about his time in the hole. His first theory was that the officials at Stalag XVIIIC had no idea that some of the Nazi guards were committing this type of torture outside of the camp. War crimes were rampant, he reasoned, and it was entirely possible that some guards administered their own style of justice. His second theory was that the officials at Stalag XVIIIC knew exactly what was going on and simply didn't care about the actions of the ruthless Nazi guards. Unfortunately, he never found out the truth. All he knew was that he and his friends were tortured and they all suffered terribly. "Those loyal Nazi bastards had a score to settle with any American POW who escaped while on work detail," he told my mother one night, with tears streaming down his face. "If you escaped and then were caught, you were doomed to certain misery or even death. They were damn bounty hunters, with their own type of justice."

When Dad woke up after being taken unconscious to the camp, he saw that he was in a hut similar to the one in Moosburg. Several hours had passed since he'd been removed from his appalling standing torture, and Dad had no memory of arriving here. Questions filled his mind. Soon several of the other POWs began to tell him how they'd come to his rescue after he was brought to the camp.

Trying to Forget the Hole

I uncovered the story of my dad's harrowing experience in the hole while searching through his personal papers. My mother hadn't known a lot about it. We discussed it while she was alive, but there were parts of the story she couldn't tell me. She heard about my dad's second solitary confinement only once, after he woke up from yet another flashback nightmare. But after that he'd refused to talk about it or even admit that it had really happened. My mother tried hard to get him to open up on the subject, but tears would well up in his eyes and he couldn't do it.

Dad survived his torture, but its stinging effects lingered with him until the day he died. Based on what I learned from my mother and from the transcript of the testimony he gave under oath to the Veterans Administration in 1984, I've concluded that this was the most horrific experience of my father's war. Throughout his married life Dad tried hard to erase from his memory the pain and humiliation of those twenty-four hours in the hole. I remain amazed that I never found out anything about this until thirteen years after his death. My mother told me the following:

> Your father was in so much denial about this incident that he was able to convince himself during his waking hours that the torture never happened. Looking at him by day no one would ever suspect that something so awful had happened to him during the war. Unfortunately, his dreams at night told another story. Your father could not escape what happened to him. He constantly relived his war experiences, which were locked deep inside his mind. When we were first married I started counting his nightmares and marking them on a calendar. Within several months I stopped, because he had so many of them. I finally made him seek professional medical help, but this made it even worse for him. After trying several doctors and sleeping drugs, one doctor suggested that he fight back by going into a small closet, turning off the lights, closing the door, and shouting over and over, "This never

happened to me!" Your father was told to do this for ten minutes every day until his nightmares subsided. To me it was a load of crap. It was a very sad time for him. Even the sleeping pills could not quell his dreams. After he took them he would instantly fall asleep, but soon another horrible dream would jar him awake. The sleeping pills accentuated his dreams and greatly increased their frequency. They made it harder to wake him up because he was so lethargic and mentally out of it. Your dad suffered a great deal to keep America free at a personal cost to himself, and for that he is a hero to me.

While listening to my mother, I suddenly remembered that summer day in 1962 when I had asked her out at the clothesline about my father being a POW. She'd bent down and looked me squarely in the eyes, telling me the same thing—that my father was a hero. My mother was sensitive and insightful, and I agree with her view of my father. It took us more than a year of meeting to discuss my father's war experiences for her to finally be comfortable telling me the story of his time in the hole. I remember her repeatedly fighting tears as she recalled what my father had been through and her own sorrowful memories of how he suffered after he came home from the war. Every time he had a nightmare, the scab on his mental war wound would be ripped off, reviving his pain. He could not escape it.

But my mother had suffered as well. When he first came home from the war and they got married, she had no idea what her new husband had been through. She became more and more horrified as the truth emerged. For countless hours over three years I listened intently as my mother unraveled the mysteries of my father. I look back on that time and think of my mom as a dam about to burst. She couldn't stop or slow down, and the stories poured out of her, growing in intensity and emotion. I'm certain this was good for her. She often mentioned how happy she was that I was taking the time to better understand my father. Retelling his stories was also an immense help to her as she attempted to come to terms with his past.

I believe it is likely that my dad's torture at Stalag XVIIIC was carried out by depraved Nazi guards who were able to administer their own twisted punishment, unnoticed far away from the gates of the camp. The Nazis who tortured my dad were the same animals who'd captured him on his second escape and followed him all the way to Austria. I was able to figure out from my research and from discussions with historians in Germany and elsewhere that torturing POWs by making them stand in a deep hole was not a documented practice. But this type of torture was used extensively inside concentration camps, where inmates who gave the Nazis grief were placed in standing cells for up to seventy-two hours at a time. What amazed me the most, though, was that not one historian ever doubted my father's story. They all agreed that it was possible and had most likely happened, even if there is no widespread documentation in support of the practice and his story.

After my mom's death in June 2007, I was in charge of dismantling the life they'd built together over forty-eight years of marriage. I found some documents carefully concealed in a large leather binder. Dad had created a secret pocket in the binder. In it I found a transcription of testimony he gave under oath to a Veterans Administration doctor in 1984 who'd been helping him deal with forty years of mental anguish. The story is brief and to the point on the subject of the hole, and it also includes other details of his war experiences.

Dad and the other POWs who'd been tortured with him had been placed on the bare wooden floor of an unused shed. Dad was severely dehydrated, starving, and delirious, and his legs and ankles were swollen from standing in place for so long. Several POWs had watched him being dragged into the camp and came to his immediate aid, giving him sips of water and introducing small amounts of food. They also elevated his legs to help reduce the swelling in his ankles. It took several hours, but finally he was coherent again and beginning to ask for more water. As soon as he had his fill, he'd immediately drift off to sleep again.

The next day my father's health continued to improve, although it took several days for the swelling in his legs to disappear, and he remained terribly hungry. Dad began to converse freely with the other POWs, many of whom had no idea what had happened to him. They were deeply shocked when they heard his story.

THE TRUTH ABOUT THE WAR IS REVEALED

Dad was learning from the others that the Allies were winning the war, and it would all soon be over. This was exciting news, and he wanted to hear every word of every conversation on the subject. In the last eight months all he'd been told by the Nazis was that the United States and its allies were losing every battle. Dad began to ask more and more questions, trying to get as much information as possible. He was also anxious to find out how Bert and Stephen were faring and where they were in the camp.

An American POW told Dad that Stalag XVIIIC had established a great communication network and that he thought he could help Dad find his friends. Soon he learned that Stephen had been placed within the camp's British enclave and Bert was in another section of the American camp. The Nazis had wanted to make sure that these guys were not going to hatch a plot to escape together ever again.

My father was now back to his old self, and for the first time in months he was excited. It seemed that the rumors were real that the Allies were winning the war and drawing closer to the camp. Dad found out that most of the Nazi SS guards were leaving to stay one step ahead of the approaching Allies. In fact, the camp was slowly unraveling at the seams. The POWs remained cautious, however, worrying that the Nazi guards still in the camp might escalate their abuse of the POWs if things were not going well for the German Army.

One day, just as promised by the American POW, Dad learned the exact location of his two friends. Because of the lax controls now prevalent within the camp, Dad was able to walk over to the other side and reunite with Bert and Stephen.

It was a happy and emotional reunion, according to my mother. The men hugged one another and exchanged stories. Bert, as usual, had a lot to say, quipping about the numerous dreams he'd had after his premature rescue from the hole. Soon Dad and Stephen were roaring with laughter as Bert explained that he'd been in a tropical resort surrounded by beautiful topless girls who were feeding him whatever he wanted. But when he'd awakened from his dream, Bert's actual situation had been stark and all too real. He was on the floor of a dirty hut, doubled over in extreme pain caused by dysentery, and a lone unidentified POW was coming to his assistance.

The laughter changed to sadness as the conversation returned to the reality of the situation they'd been placed in. Bert had been so sick with diarrhea that if he hadn't been removed from the hole immediately, he would have died. The Nazi guard chosen to check on the men during their hours of torture had shown a glimmer of compassion when he noticed Bert in extreme distress and decided to remove him.

Now the conversation changed to talk of their coming liberation. Rumors were flying that the Allies were liberating camps to the north in Germany and that Nazi Germany was on the run. This explained why the SS guards were leaving the camp. My father now dreamed constantly of liberation and the food he would eat when he returned to America. When he spoke of this, he learned that the other POWs were consumed by the same thoughts. Every conversation between the POWs was now about food. My father copied into his POW journal some of the recipes the men discussed together.

At this point in his imprisonment my father had lost almost sixty-five pounds due to starvation and abuse. His face was round and swollen, his once sparkling eyes had dark circles around them, his hair was matted and dull, and his skin was very dry and rough. Dad was constantly pulling his pants up because the journal tucked inside his pants at the belt line could no longer hold them up.

As spring advanced the days were growing longer. The bored and hungry POWs spent most of their time soaking up the sun's rays. Everyone now believed they were going to survive and return home. Even extremely pessimistic Bert understood that freedom was just around the corner. This pleased my father and Stephen, because Bert had become positive for the first time since June 1944. It seemed that the horrors and brutalities they'd all experienced over the last eight months were truly behind them.

———

Back in America, my dad's family and my mother had no indication that anything had changed with my father's POW situation. All of them, including the U.S. Army and the Red Cross, still believed Dad was at Stalag VIIA in Moosburg, Germany. Based on my research, Stalag VIIA still believed that prisoner number 89 114, Herbert H Miller, was living in dismal hut 7A. This is why no record was ever found of my father's time in Stalag XVIIIC. Because of their escape, Dad and the others had now officially vanished into the unknown. That in itself was a scary situation that could have led to devastating results for their families if something tragic had happened to the men.

As the days went by Dad and his friends were running out of things to talk about. Despite this, they still came together every day to enjoy each other's companionship. The food situation was spiraling downward. Dad refused to drink the black tea anymore because it upset his stomach. He told my mother the camp soup looked like liquid poop and smelled even worse. The hungry and hopeful POWs were growing very edgy.

THE WAR ENDS AND THE CAMP GOES WILD

On May 8, 1945, the news that the war was finally over swept through the camp. "Boy, you never seen anyone happier in your entire life than all of us POWs!" wrote my father in his journal. Hearing the news, the peppery Stephen just smiled and said, "Thank God!" Bert cried uncontrollably for more than an hour. Bert was shedding all of the emotional baggage he'd been holding on tightly to since the beginning of the war. My father was also moved to tears. After their initial feelings of exuberant euphoria, he and the other POWs sank into exhaustion from the relief of not having to worry about living in peril every moment of their lives. For the first time in eleven months, my father felt safe and believed that his horrific experiences were now behind him.

Nervousness now overcame my father as he thought about his impending liberation. The fear that this liberation wasn't really going to happen began to overwhelm him. After all, over the past months countless situations had never materialized or had gone wrong with devastating results. "What if this is not true? What if it becomes delayed?" my father was thinking.

War can alter the human spirit and change your life forever. Unfortunately, my father's post-traumatic stress symptoms began just hours after he received the news of his impending liberation. Gone was the incredible stress of the war, the constant overriding fears of death and torture. New fears now started to take hold of his life and would be present in him until his death nearly fifty years later.

My father wrote the following in his journal: "You could see a big change around Markt Pongau and this hell hole Stalag XVIIIC. Now the Jerries [Nazis] were leaving and the Yankees [Allied troops] were coming. The war ended on May 8, 1945. The next day we cut all the wire down around the camp and cut a large hole in the security fence so we could venture out into the countryside. There was no holding us GI's in anymore! Some of the stronger men went up into the hills and killed some sheep and brought them back to the camp."

All of the Nazi guards were now gone. The POWs were coming and going through the hole in the fence whenever they wanted, including at all hours of the night. Dad reported that pandemonium and chaos reigned—everyone in the camp was acting like kids with no supervision. Some of the men began to gorge themselves on roasted lamb. Others were unable to control their emotions and were acting like fools. Two medical doctors among the POWs ran frantically around the camp warning the men not to gorge themselves with meat or any food that was out of the ordinary until the Red Cross arrived. Doing this could seriously jeopardize their lives, the doctors explained, to no avail in a few instances. Dad and Bert heeded the warnings, remembering how sick they'd become when they ate too much after being starved on their 1,325-kilometer march to Moosburg. Stephen took the advice of my father and Bert, refraining from the urge to overeat.

Unfortunately two men in Dad's hut did not listen to the doctors' advice. The men became sicker by the minute and suffered agonizing deaths. Reports of other men dying from overeating went through the camp. Dad did take a mouthful of lamb, but it made him sick to his stomach.

THE ALLIES AND THE RED CROSS ARRIVE

On May 12, 1945, the Allied forces drove their tanks and trucks through the front gate of Stalag XVIIIC. Nine months and six days after becoming a prisoner of war, my father was living in freedom again. He, Bert, Stephen, and the other POWs cried with jubilation. My father recalled that he sat on the ground, with the bright sun warming his back, and watched events unfold. A mass of wild, cheering, jubilant soldiers swarmed the Allies. Now they all were officially free. From that moment on the American POWs were GIs once again.

Within several hours the Red Cross appeared at the camp with trucks and supplies for the men. They entered and explored the surroundings, becoming increasingly dismayed by conditions in the camp. One Red Cross official said, "Every camp we've entered is filled with atrocities, death, and sadness." Bert told him: "The Nazis were the worst hosts ever. They treated us like shit, the place smelled like shit, and our experiences were like shit. There you have it, a totally shitty experience." Hearing this, the men roared with laughter. It even brought a smile to some of the Red Cross personnel. It was good to hear laughter again, and now the mood in the camp was more like a circus than a POW camp.

After the initial excitement subsided, my father began to realize that he wasn't feeling well. Dad had a slight fever, and his body ached all over. As usual, he'd been ignoring his symptoms, denying to himself that something was wrong. Had he eaten spoiled food? he wondered. Was it the mouthful of lamb? He lay down on his bed; later that day the Red Cross paid a visit. The Red Cross personnel could see immediately that the white parts of my father's eyes were slightly yellow. His skin also looked yellow. Quickly assessing his condition, a Red Cross official diagnosed "possible jaundice." Dad was in total shock.

Dad was instructed to get outside in the sun as much as possible over the next several days. Many other men had also developed the same condition, and they were told it was caused by malnutrition and a lack of vitamin D. After a few days of being out in the sunshine and eating better food, Dad's jaundice began to subside. He was now sunburned, but it was a lot better than looking yellow.

The Red Cross was in charge now, and they were confronting enormous individual issues among the GIs. Their first concern was getting enough food into the camp so that the men could start eating normal meals again. The second was addressing the multitude of critical health issues. Many of the men were severely malnourished and hadn't taken in enough food or calories in a long while. Once again the Red Cross warned the GIs that overeating could cause them serious health complications or death. My father and his friends were in this special group of men, and all were being fed small amounts of popcorn to accustom their stomachs to food again. Popcorn was made available for several days, and each GI was encouraged to eat it throughout the day. My father loved popcorn, so this was a real treat.

THE FORMER POWS LEAVE FOR FRANCE

On Friday May 18, 1945, Bert, Stephen, my father, and hundreds of other former POWs officially left Stalag XVIIIC and headed to one of the many "cigarette" camps located on the western shores of France. Extremely happy, Dad and his friends could hardly contain their excitement. The entire camp was acting like a circus had rolled into town. My father grabbed his war journal, relic, and dog tags and placed them into the green army-issued pack that each GI had received from the Red Cross. Looking down at the dog tags in his hand, Dad had to decide if he should leave the ones from Stalag VIIA behind. Many of the GIs were discarding the Stalag dog tags as cruel reminders of what they had been through over the past months. Dad started to remove his from the chain, but decided he'd keep them as a reminder of the hell he'd been through. Perhaps someday he would show them to Eleanore and his future children and tell them his story.

According to my mother, my father also thought about discarding his war journal but quickly realized this would be a very stupid mistake. Proud of the journal, he cherished its contents because they reminded him of Heinz and the special friendship they'd shared. Ironically, sharing anything from his war with his two children was never to happen. My father's post-traumatic stress started the moment he became a free man. Dad's war experiences were too harrowing and painful for him to ever share with anyone other than my mother.

As Bert, Stephen, and Dad boarded the truck that would take them to Salzburg, memories started flowing through my father's mind. It had been an incredible life-altering ten months. The reality of being free of POW life and Nazi atrocities and on his way home to America was overwhelming for him.

Sitting down on the truck's wooden benches, Dad shifted his thoughts to wondering what had happened to Heinz. Feeling sad, he knew he would always miss his good friend. Tears welled up as he remembered the many times Heinz helped him and the others, often putting his own life in jeopardy. My mother told me Dad was convinced it was because of Heinz's heroic efforts from the moment of his capture that he and the others had survived.

Many other thoughts were also running through my father's mind. Dad had met so many special European people during this war, people who while displaced from their families unselfishly put their lives on the line for the Allies. Dad especially remembered the small French man who had come to their rescue with homemade cake and honey, when he and others were starving during their terrible march to Moosburg. This memory made him smile. My father was proud that he'd helped to eradicate the tyrant Adolf Hitler and crush his Nazi war machine, even though his efforts had come with a high emotional cost to himself.

The truck started up and prepared to move out toward Salzburg. Thick black smoke emitted by the growling diesel engulfed the back of the truck, reminding some of the men of the smoke from dropping bombs during the war. Laughing now, my father noticed some of the more impatient GIs cursing the smoke and wondering out loud why the truck hadn't been started before they climbed on board.

Here are the words of my father as they appeared in his journal: "We are finally leaving Markt Pongau by truck heading for Salzburg, Austria! The trip will take about four hours to complete due to the various detours we will need to make around areas that were destroyed by the war. From there we will be all loaded on C-47's and flown to La Havre,

France, to Camp Lucky Strike." The trip was uneventful and even wonderful, according to my mother. This was the only trip in my father's wartime career that was not strafed by gunfire, dropping bombs, or hostile enemy fire. Nobody died or was wounded. As they arrived at the airfield in Salzburg and loaded onto the planes for departure, my father enjoyed seeing the many thousands of POWs just like himself who were being transported away from the camps to be processed, deloused, and eventually sent home. The excitement continued to build for my father and his friends.

The massive C-47 lifted off and began to gain altitude. Dad was lucky enough to be near one of the few windows on the plane. All the GIs near this window were trying to get a quick look at the war-ravaged countryside far below. Finally it was my father's turn. He peered out the window, and it took a moment for his eyes to adjust to the bright sunny day. The first thing Dad noticed was the devastation from so many battles. He saw a moderate-sized city that had been almost completely destroyed. He told my mother shortly after arriving back in America that it had been horrible seeing destroyed tanks, trucks, and leveled towns. Europe was a mess, with many of its cities nearly obliterated.

Dad relinquished his spot and let Stephen have a look. Stephen gazed through the window, saying nothing. Pulling his head back, he turned as if to speak to my father but changed his mind, quickly returning his gaze to the window. "Those bloody motherfuckers!" Stephen finally said, referring to the Nazis and the carnage and destruction they'd spread throughout Western Europe. Bert was next. He glanced below at the passing countryside and returned to his seat without saying a word. This is the first and only time my dad had ever known Bert to be speechless. The scene below had really upset him. Dad instantly understood that Bert was now very thankful and amazed that he'd somehow managed to survive.

CAMP LUCKY STRIKE

The plane ride took just under two hours, and finally the group touched down at Camp Lucky Strike. Camp Lucky, as it was commonly called, was the central collection point for all American and Allied forces that had been taken prisoner during the war. The enormous camp was so big that they'd had to create an extra makeshift airstrip on the grass to accommodate the planes arriving from all over Europe. When my father got there, he joined 3,000 other GIs, and more were coming in by the hour. A tent city close to the sea, Camp Lucky had been carved out of the French countryside near the town of Le Havre. All day long planes were coming and going to bring the food, cigarettes, and supplies that were needed to help the GIs recover from life as a POW.

Dad and his friends stepped off the plane and were immediately told to strip. Soon they were taking long hot-as-you-want showers and being deloused, because their clothes were loaded with mites, fleas, and bedbugs. Each GI was given two sets of new uniforms, and their old ones were burned. All were also supplied with plenty of hot food to help them begin to regain the weight they'd lost. The best part of the camp was the unlimited amount of cigarettes available to the men; hence the name "Camp Lucky Strike." The next day my father and the others received complete physical exams, and if they had a medical condition, it was treated immediately. My father's jaundice had disappeared, just as the Red Cross personnel had said it would, and this made him even happier.

For the next three weeks my father's only responsibility was to eat, rest, smoke, and recover from his ordeal, while the army obtained his military records from the United States. Each man was debriefed and asked many questions about his POW experiences. This was very hard for Bert and my father. Stephen, on the other hand, was feisty and direct and made no bones about hating the "motherfucking Nazis." He supplied so much information to the American and British armies that they finally had to cut him off so they could get stories from the others.

FAREWELL TO STEPHEN

Soon it was time for Stephen to leave Camp Lucky and return home to England. Stephen was sufficiently recuperated, but it was really hard for Bert and my father to see him go. My father told my mother: "It was a bittersweet time seeing our friend leave to resume his life back in England. We had survived the hell together and been good friends throughout our ordeal. Now it was time for all of us to return to our own countries and homes." My father's lower lip quivered in sadness, and he fought back the tears, as he and Bert said their final goodbyes to Stephen. They exchanged addresses, Stephen giving Bert and Dad his mother's in England.

Several years later, right after my sister Debbie was born, my father tried to contact Stephen. The three letters Dad sent over nine months were eventually returned, marked "No Such Address." My father was devastated and wondered what had happened to his good friend. "This bothered your dad very much," my mother told me. "He acted like it didn't, but I could see the grief in his eyes. Your dad eventually told me he really needed to see Stephen."

My father to his dying day never heard from Stephen again. Nobody has any idea what happened to him. My father's last memory of Stephen was of waving goodbye to him as his plane lifted off from Camp Lucky Strike in France, on June 9, 1945. May God bless Stephen. I know my father would have wanted me to say this. So I'm breaking the rules of writing and doing it now. Thank you, Stephen, for being a friend to my dad. Your friendship and support during the bleakest of times helped my father to become a truly remarkable man.

OFF TO AMERICA,
WHERE DAD AND BERT SAY GOODBYE

The paperwork for Bert and my dad finally arrived from the U.S. on June 9. Everything was in order, and the next day Bert and Dad headed home on a Liberty ship. During the voyage they were inseparable. Meanwhile, telegrams from my father were arriving at the homes of Eleanore and his parents. To his parents, he wrote, "I LOVE YOU, RETURNING HOME SOON, I HAVE A SURPRISE!" My mother recited to me from memory what he wrote to her: "I LOVE YOU! WILL BE HOME SOON. WILL YOU MARRY ME?"

I had no idea that my father proposed to my mother in a war telegram. The original telegram was lost after the war when they moved from Detroit into our house in Dearborn. My mom always regretted losing the telegram. I heard this story from my mother one week before she was critically injured in an automobile accident, which killed her six weeks later. I've learned since that getting married fast after the war was common among GIs. Many returned with an enhanced appreciation for life, and my father was no different. After my mother told me this story, I realized that I'd never once asked either one of my parents how they'd decided to get married.

My mom also told me that the U. S. Army War Department had sent a telegram to my father's parents when the Red Cross discovered him in Stalag XVIIIC, announcing that he was liberated and safe in their hands. Everyone had been astonished to hear that he was now in another camp. When my mother found out that he was safe and coming home, she made up her mind to marry him.

———

It took Bert and my father eight days to make it back to America from the coast of France. This time the voyage was sunny, with no rain whatsoever. It was a notable contrast from the trip to Scotland the year before. Dad was nervous with anticipation and thinking about how he and Bert would soon be parting to start their new lives as war veterans and civilians. During the voyage Dad had made up his mind that he was not returning to live in West Virginia. His new home would be in Detroit, Michigan, with Eleanore, where employment opportunities would be better than in his home state. Meanwhile, my mother was making plans to see my father as soon as he arrived back in America; she was going to suggest an August wedding date.

When the Liberty ship moored in Boston Harbor, excitement filled the air and the entire city of Boston was alive with celebration. Bert and Dad came off the ship and the moment he touched American soil, my dad began to cry with joy. According to my mother, who heard this story directly from Bert, tears were streaming down my father's face as he bent down on one knee, saluted our flag, kissed the ground, and thanked God for a safe return. Truly it was a miracle that Bert and my father had survived the war. Soon both men were placed inside Camp Miles Standish, and immediate plans were made for them to return home.

———

The following day my father faced a four-hour debriefing, with the army requesting all the details. My father understood the necessity for the debriefing, but it ripped off the scabs on his memory, and once again he was reliving every horrible detail of his POW life. Sadness permeated the room as my father told his stories. He recalled that they'd needed to replace the stenographer after she became overwhelmed with grief and sadness. My mother firmly believed to her dying day that this debriefing was the root cause of why my father could never again open up about his POW experiences. Unfortunately, in 1945 there were no counselors or mental health support groups available. My father had to tough it out alone under a barrage of questions from government officials. When they were finished, Dad was thanked for his heroic service to and sacrifice on behalf of the United States of America.

After the debriefing, my father was a mental wreck. Bert, too, was so sad he didn't want to return to West Virginia, fearing that his parents would think he was a "softy."

Several days later, the men were given liberty to go out and have fun in Boston. Fun is certainly what they all had. After a big drinking night, complete with massive hangovers, Bert and my father were returned by train to Camp Atterbury in Indiana, where they would be reunited with their parents.

When the train arrived at Camp Atterbury, it was time for Bert and my father to part. Dad would be traveling east to Wheeling, West Virginia, and Bert to somewhere near Charleston, in the southern part of the state. It was a sad moment for both men, who had relied on each other so much that other GIs referred to them as "Mutt and Jeff." My father once again fought back the tears as he said his goodbyes to Bert. And Bert was too overcome with emotion to speak. Bert did manage to choke out the following: "Herb, without your friendship, leadership, and understanding, I could never have survived this horrible war and made it back here alive." Dad was moved as they hugged. "It was certainly an adventure, Bert, to say the least," my father told him. And then, just as they had done on their second escape from the Stalag work detail in Munich, Bert and Dad walked away from each other while saying goodbye. My father had the same broad smile as before, and, this time, so did Bert. But Bert was not going to be changing his mind and joining my father. Those times were gone forever.

REUNION

Walking toward the camp gates, my father paused for a moment to collect his thoughts and regain his composure. This was it. The terrible war was now over for him. This was the moment he'd dreamed about and longed for as a prisoner of war in Nazi Germany. Vivid details from the events of the past year flooded his mind as he prepared to meet his family.

Dad remembered the French family he'd befriended and buried; the army's bizarre mistakes that almost got him killed in Operation Cobra; the brutal two-month march to Moosburg; the terrifying train trips from the POW camp to Munich and back; his two failed escapes; and the gruesome torture he'd endured. But he also remembered the kindness and humanity of the French people; the wonderful Christmas celebration in the POW camp; and, most poignant of all, his friendship with Heinz, the compassionate and principled German guard, whom he would mourn for the rest of his life.

Now putting a big smile on his face, Dad exited the gates of Camp Atterbury and looked around for his family. His determination to survive and return home to Eleanore and his family had kept him going. With his heart pounding out of his chest, he waited for his mother, father, and two sisters to appear (his brother, Hank, was still in the Pacific).

Dad could hear the screams and cries of other families reuniting with their GIs. Above the clamor, he also heard a female voice calling,

"Herbert, Herbert, Herbert." A strikingly beautiful girl began running toward him with outstretched arms. "Herbert, I love you," she yelled. Coming into focus was the lovely face in the picture he'd taped inside his T-shirt and worn next to his heart for an entire year. Totally shocked at the sight of his sweetheart, Dad could see past her to his family beaming with joy and pride.

Without hesitation, my mother ran into my father's arms. Tears of joy streamed down her face as she kissed him repeatedly. They hadn't seen each other in eighteen months. It was clear my mother wasn't going to let him get away ever again. Dad's parents had tears in their eyes as they witnessed the reunion of the young lovers. Within moments, the entire family surrounded the embracing couple, and Dad's homecoming celebration was under way.

BERT AND DAD REUNITE IN 1947

Once they were back in America, not a day passed that Dad didn't think of his pal Bert. He remembered fondly how Bert had summoned wit and humor to get them through both the tedium and the horror of POW life. Dad was especially concerned about Bert's adjustment to civilian life, hoping that his POW experiences hadn't caused him any lasting problems. They exchanged several letters and chose a date for a much-anticipated reunion. It would take place in the summer of 1947, two years after the end of the war. They planned to meet in West Virginia when my parents were visiting my grandparents in Wheeling.

My father and mother were happily married and living in Detroit in a two-story flat. Bert was engaged and living in an isolated mountain town south of Charleston, West Virginia. Bert met my parents at a roadside diner in a small town halfway between Wheeling and Charleston. During the drive south, my father was full of anticipation. The closer they came to their destination, though, the quieter my father became. My mother knew he was mulling over many of the events he and Bert had shared during the war. She could tell from the look on my father's face that this was hard for him.

When they walked into the diner, it was easy to spot Bert because the restaurant was almost empty. He was sitting by himself sipping a cup of coffee while patiently awaiting my father's arrival. Bert spied him and jumped up from the table, knocking over his chair. It was just like Bert,

The Chicken Caper

Dad liked chicken and lots of it. I remember the story my uncle and mom told me about my dad going to Frankenmuth, Michigan, to eat at Zehnder's, the world-famous German restaurant that serves family-style chicken dinners. Zehnder's was known at the time for promoting all-you-can-eat meals.

Just back from the war, Dad took a Sunday drive two hours north with Mom and members of their extended families to Frankenmuth. My father was still not back to his normal weight after his POW experience, when he'd lost more than sixty-five pounds, and he was hungry that day. He and my uncle ate so much chicken that the manager at Zehnder's finally came to the table to inform them that the all-you-can-eat meal was over for them.

Everyone at the table burst out laughing. They all knew my dad had become an eating machine. It was common for my mom to make up to ten sandwiches for his lunch every day. It took almost two years for his appetite to return to normal and for him to regain the weight he'd lost in the war. My mom was glad when she was finally able to send him off to work with only two sandwiches in his lunchbox.

my dad thought, to make a scene. "You're still like a bull in a china shop," laughed Dad. He stretched out his hand to greet Bert, saying, "I'm so happy to see you my good friend." Tears filled their eyes as the two men embraced. It was also an emotional moment for my mother as she witnessed the bond of friendship that existed between the reunited buddies.

Bert and Dad immediately commented on how much fatter each had become. Dad had never seen Bert looking robust and fit. At Stalag VIIA he had appeared frail and weak. Bert was totally amazed by my father's build, although he said that Dad's face looked the same except that his formerly dull and lifeless eyes were now bright and sparkling with freedom. The two men realized they'd never seen each other at a normal weight. Bert and Dad's friendship had developed during their 1,325-kilometer march to Stalag VIIA as their weight spiraled downward from starvation.

After the initial hugs and laughs, Dad introduced Bert to my mother (his fiancée had not been able to come because of a family situation). They sat down at the table and told their life stories from the last two years. What a marvelous time they had that day, laughing, crying, and reminiscing about the hardships and bittersweet times they'd shared as prisoners of Nazi Germany. Bert made sure my mother knew just how lovesick my father had been without her and how neat he thought it was that Dad had carried her picture taped inside his T-shirt next to his heart. Bert joked that my father had never changed his T-shirt over the entire eleven months.

Knowing that my father was still grieving for his German friend, Bert reminded him that Heinz had been a great man who'd helped all of them to survive. They also talked about Stephen and how much they missed their feisty English pal who hadn't been afraid to challenge the Nazis. Soon the discussion turned to their two escapes and the torture they'd endured from the Nazis.

It was becoming clear to my parents that Bert now detested anyone who was of German descent. My father did not share Bert's feeling. Dad hated the Nazi regime and all that it had stood for. But he didn't hate the German people. He reminded Bert that many thousands of German people had felt displaced within their own country, living under Hitler while detesting his beliefs. He also reminded Bert of the compassionate German civilian in Munich who'd helped them escape the first time by letting them into his barn. And he mentioned Heinz again. Unfortunately Bert was having trouble separating anger from reality. My father finally dropped the subject and steered the conversation in a new direction, hoping his friend would one day change his attitude toward the German people.

As Bert talked, Dad looked into his eyes and remembered how hard it had been for Bert to see beyond the barbed-wire fences that had encircled the prison camp. He'd always believed he was doomed to die. It took months of coaching and encouragement to get Bert to "see" through the fences and dream of being free again. The fierce anger he was dealing with now was clouding his judgment.

My mom could see that this reunion with his war buddy was good for my dad. But soon it was time for Dad and Bert to say goodbye. In the back of their minds they surely understood that it was going to be difficult to maintain their tight bond as family responsibilities, jobs, and other commitments began to take over their lives. My mother said it was a sad moment when Dad and Bert said goodbye that day in the West Virginia diner. Each had changed emotionally since returning to America and leaving the army. Gone was the commonality of opinions they had shared in Europe. Bert was nursing anger, hostility, and regret in his effort to subdue the horrors of his war. My father, on the other hand, had very little hate left over from his war but retained plenty of emotional wounds and scars.

Shortly before her death in 2007, my mother told me about the drive back to Wheeling that day. The conversation on that drive stayed with her for the rest of her life. "When Bert, Stephen, and I were in the war together," my father told my mother, "we all had pretty much the same beliefs and feelings about the war. The common factor between us was our goal to survive and return home." But now that they had accomplished this great goal, my dad explained, they were moving forward in their lives and living safe and free in their own towns. "It is amazing to me how our perspectives and attitudes can change over time," he said. He made my mother promise that she would never let him become hateful toward anyone because of his war experiences. "I never want to hate anyone or carry around pent-up hostility," he told her. "I don't want you living with a hate-filled husband." My mother had been so impressed and proud of my father for being able to say that to her. She told me that she had understood the situation completely.

I never knew my father to hate anyone. He never shed his emotional scars or truly came to terms with his experiences in the war. But adding anger and hatred to those scars would only have destroyed the man he had become.

Bert and my father spoke on the phone several times over the years. But like paint on an old barn, their friendship slowly faded away. Thirty years later my father became active in his 30th Infantry Division association and attended his army reunions, reuniting with many of his war friends. Unfortunately, after the last of those phone calls, my father never heard from Bert again.

EPILOGUE

Writing this book has been a fantastic emotional journey for me and one of the most rewarding experiences of my life. I've spent countless hours in search of my father's war, visiting European sites, meeting historians, and talking with people who are knowledgeable about World War II. Because I travel to Europe every month for my work as an automotive technology and lighting design consultant, more than half of the book was written on location in England, France, and Germany. I was able to coordinate my work schedule with my book schedule and visit all the places where my father spent time during the war. This has given me a special perspective, bringing me much closer to my father and his experiences. Along the way, I forged many new and lasting friendships.

On a day in May 2009 I am amazed to receive a phone call from my good friend Noel Sarrazin, who is president of the 30th Infantry Division, European Association, and lives in Mortain, France. He informs me that he has placed my name on the master list of special dignitaries for the Sixty-Fifth Anniversary of D-Day commemoration ceremony on Omaha Beach. Noel has decided that I qualify for a special invite, telling me to expect a joint invitation from American president Barack Obama and French president Nicholas Sarkozy. I am thrilled and honored to realize how much my new French friends admire my father and my passion for writing his story. A few weeks later, just as Noel has promised,

I receive my invitation from the White House via e-mail. It is a terrific moment.

I begin to plan my trip, deciding to devote four days to the festivities in Normandy. My first stop will be in Mortain, where my dad's fellow 30th Infantry soldier and good friend Frank W. Towers, an energetic ninety-two-year-old, is going to be awarded the highest honor France can bestow on a U.S. citizen, the Legion of Honor Medal.

———

Arriving in France, I pick up a rental car at the train station in Caen. I head for Mortain, navigating for several hours along narrow and winding roads through the beautiful French countryside. I am filled with excitement as I approach Mortain, a town I've grown to love over six visits in just two years. I can't wait to see the many new friends I've made there. I push the accelerator to the floor and shift my car into fifth gear, easily accelerating up the steep tree-lined hills. The music of Lonesome Dove is streaming through the car's speakers, adding to my good mood. It occurs to me that the sentinel of impressively large trees creating a beautiful canopy of vegetation over my head must have survived the great battle of Mortain over sixty-five years ago. I enter the center of town, its quaint buildings lining the road tightly, and turn toward another steep hill that will take me to Hill 314, where my father became a prisoner of Nazi Germany.

Today I am meeting Noel Sarrazin at a joyful celebration on the top of Hill 314, next to the chapel (now a monument) where my father came to pray and found the religious relic he carried throughout the war. Here 950 men from the 30th Division gave their lives to liberate France from Nazi Germany. Frank Towers was instrumental in erecting the beautiful black marble monument in honor of the men of the 30th Division.

The Legion of Honor Medal is pinned to Frank's lapel, and the 300 people gathered on the hill begin to cheer. Frank has spent the last forty years of his life fostering good will and keeping the bonds between America and France strong. Now France is honoring him for his heartfelt efforts.

After the ceremony, Mortain resident Michel Paysant pulls up in a restored World War II U.S. Army jeep, complete with every amenity, and offers me a ride. I bang my knees as I jump in, amazed by the extremely tight fit between the seats and the dashboard. I can't believe how small the inside of the jeep is. We pull away from the chapel and the crowd, and soon I am on my father's journey. The ride is rough and bumpy, even on smooth ground, but the old jeep easily picks up speed. We arrive at the parking area overlooking the farmhouse and well where my father was taken prisoner. I try to imagine what it must have been like for my father as he sat in his jeep on August 6, 1944, just moments before his unfortunate encounter with the Nazis.

Now it's my turn to drive. Changing seats, I instinctively push the clutch to the floor and shift into first gear. Soon we are passing the farmhouse, and it looks much as it did in 1944. I can see the well my father visited, its long pump handle towering over the thick meadow grass. The scenery here is breathtaking, and the early evening sunshine and warm temperatures are the same weather conditions my father experienced when he was taken prisoner. I am about as close as I'm going to get to his experience. I pass the farm and realize that it was on this spot that my father took his last breath as a free man for nine months. My eyes begin to well up as I savor this special adventure in honor of my father.

We drive back to the chapel, where the crowd is thinning. Noel and a group of French dignitaries invite me to join them in a champagne toast to Frank Towers and all the men of the 30th Division. Frank turns to me, raises his glass high, and toasts my father's memory and the event that forever changed his life. I am humbled and feeling very proud of my father.

The next day I return to Paris for a business meeting. As soon as it ends, I drive back to Normandy for more D-Day festivities. On the afternoon of June 5, I arrive at Noel Sarrazin's stunning French farmhouse. I feel like I am driving up to a photo in *Better Homes and Gardens* magazine. We are quickly off to Utah Beach for the evening's events. Arriving near

Utah Beach, I am totally amazed to see hundreds of U.S. Army jeeps, all-terrain vehicles, trucks, and tanks, all restored and in perfect condition. Thousands of people are streaming into the area dressed as U.S., British, French, and Canadian World War II soldiers. The air is filled with fun and anticipation, and I have an eerie sense that we are all back in June 1944.

I walk among the crowd, camera in hand, and observe ten World War II vets who stormed onto this very beach sixty-five years ago. All have made the long trip across the Atlantic, and every one of them, beaming with pride and excitement, is being treated like a hero. It is a magic evening. I am introduced to Helen Patton, granddaughter of General George S. Patton. My father served under (way under) General Patton. Helen's presence and her commitment to keeping her grandfather's spirit alive in Western Europe is inspiring. When I speak with her, I can clearly see the fire in her eyes and the passion she has for freedom. She is proud of her grandfather and everything he stood for.

The evening ends with a spectacular fifty-mile-long fireworks display extending along the Normandy coast, from the Cotentin Peninsula to Caen. As I look in either direction I see fireworks exploding over each of the five beaches that the Allies landed on all those years ago. I close my eyes and listen to the thunderous bombardment, trying to imagine what it must have been like to hear the explosions on the beaches in 1944. I am completely safe and enjoying a wonderful social evening. But I'm thinking about the men who came here to liberate France, facing utter peril and putting their lives on the line. I open my eyes to once again take in the beauty of the fireworks. I remain in awe of the vast reach of the effort put forth on that day sixty-five years ago. I am so proud to be present at this occasion.

The day I've been waiting for, Saturday, June 6, finally arrives. Noel and I leave his house with his wife, Marie-Claire, and daughter, Anne, and travel to Caen to board a bus for the trip to the American Cemetery in Colleville-sur-Mer. We are on our way to the Sixty-Fifth Anniversary of

D-Day commemoration ceremony. When we arrive, I gaze at the 9,387 stunning white crosses that dot the graves of the American soldiers who lost their lives on June 6, 1944. I am overcome with emotion. Men like my father came here and unselfishly risked everything, because freedom was worth dying for. My father was incredibly lucky to survive.

Now, sixty-five years later, the wind is slight, the sun burns brightly, and the smell of flowers permeates the fresh ocean air. I take my seat with the other 7,000 invited guests, wishing my family could be with me. I pull out my iPhone and text-message Colleen and our youngest son, Patrick, to tell them I'm here and the location of my seat so they can look for me on TV. Within seconds, Patrick connects and we begin to share this experience together.

A steady stream of dignitaries pours onto the enormous stage. The leaders of the Allied nations—France, England, Canada, and the United States—are all present. Joining them are about seventy vibrant veterans, including Frank Towers. Anchored just off the beach are two large U.S. Navy ships. They are here to protect President Obama and his fellow world leaders. Sadly, times have changed, and those ships are on guard against terrorism. I speculate that most of the people attending the ceremony believe these war ships are here in honor of the day and that nobody is thinking about terrorism.

I am dreaming once again, imagining I am here on June 6, 1944. I pretend that the navy ships I am looking at offshore signal a successful invasion. Squinting my eyes, I try even harder to imagine what it must have been like to see the overwhelming maze of ships, convoys, and soldiers. I cannot even come close to visualizing that scene. I stop daydreaming and turn my focus to the presentations and speeches.

British Prime Minister Gordon Brown is the first speaker, and his comments strike a positive note with me: "On that June morning, the young of our nations stepped out onto these beaches below me into history. As long as freedom lives their deeds will never die." His words remind me of how young my father and the other soldiers were when they came here. Those young adults were not as sophisticated as the young adults of today. They were being asked to lay down their lives for something they probably did not fully understand. My father hadn't a clue about what he was about to endure when he arrived on the shores of Omaha Beach on June 11, 1944.

Brown continues speaking, giving examples of heroism, bravery, and honor. I feel my father's presence with me at this special event. I am able to somehow visualize him on the LCI with my wife's uncle John McGuckin. My father would be nervously anticipating the impending landing and his departure from the LCI. I am certain he would have said something nice to the LCI captain before departing from the craft. It was just his way. I can see my father walking across the beach, heading for the front lines of battle. He probably looked down at his sea-soaked boots, now coated in sand, and wondered how long it would take for them to dry. I depart from my reverie to hear Brown say: "We remember those who advanced grain of sand by grain of sand to win this war."

Now firmly back in the reality of this day, I listen to the other speeches. I am feeling totally in sync with my father and connected to his memory. President Obama takes the podium to give the key-note address. My mind is no longer wandering as he says, "For three centuries no invader had ever been able to cross the English Channel into Normandy. And it had never been more difficult than in 1944. . . . The sheer improbability of this victory is part of what makes D-Day so memorable."

I turn my head to scan the beautiful American Cemetery. Each of the 9,387 marble crosses displays both an American and a French flag. I am amazed that the cemetery staff took the time to do this. Every detail of today's event has been precisely planned and polished. I am so honored to be here. I'm still thinking about those dual flags and what they represent as I recap in my mind my special relationships with the people of France's Normandy region. I've grown to love this enchanting area of the world—it has brought me so many new friends. I wonder what my father would think if he had lived to see the passionate interest I've taken in his war. My passion began, I realize, on that night many years ago when I overheard my father crying as he made a haunting comment to my mother about having been a POW. From that night on I was hooked. It would take my father's death, followed by thirteen years of talking about him with my mother, and, finally, her untimely death, to bring my passion to fruition.

A thunderous twenty-one-gun salute closes the hour-long presentation. I look around and fail to see a dry eye anywhere. Tears stream down my face as I watch four jets representing each of the Allied countries soar above us. Three of the jets split off in different directions and head toward the horizon while the fourth aims straight up into the atmosphere, to be swallowed by the sky. I can feel the pride and emotion in the air.

———————————

Now I am rousted out of my seat and told to proceed to the dignitary area near the back of the stage. My heart is beating with excitement as I move through the thousands of people trying to get a close-up of the heads of state. I am separated from Noel and his family and end up with another group of French and American friends. The crowd suddenly opens up as I approach the dignitary area. I am pushed ahead to stand directly in front of the line of presidents, prime ministers, and royalty. Feeling ever so star-struck, I find myself less than five feet from Barack Obama, Nicolas Sarkozy, Gordon Brown, and Prince Charles. Moving into the line a bit farther away is Canadian Prime Minister Stephen Harper.

My cue to move closer comes when a Secret Service agent approaches and places his hand on my shoulder, asking me to step up to meet the honored guests. President Obama greets me, and I extend my hand. He asks why I am here. My training as a business professional comes to my aid as I recount my father's entire war story in the time it takes for an elevator to travel one floor. To my delight, President Obama is clearly interested in what I have to say.

Just as I finish my summary, one of my nearby friends announces loudly that I am writing a book about my father's incredible war experiences. President Obama looks directly at me and says, "Is this true?"

"Yes," I tell him, "my father entered World War II on D-Day plus five and was captured in France by Nazi Germany. He was marched 1,325 kilometers to a Stalag prison camp in Germany," I continue, "where he endured nine hideous months as a POW. After two failed escape attempts, he was finally liberated by the Allies." President Obama responds, "Wow! I'm honored and I thank your father for his service to his country. When your book is finished, I would certainly like to read it." "Yes sir," I reply. "I will make sure you receive a copy."

I continue to travel down the line, telling my story. I come to Prince Charles, and the line stops ahead of me. I have a few extra moments with the future king of England. He has heard my previous comments and inquires about my book, expressing his interest in reading it.

I eventually break away from the crowd, feeling deeply satisfied with my day. Never in my wildest dreams had I expected to meet the leaders of four nations (not to mention a member of British royalty) and have any of them ask about my book and express an interest in reading it. While I mull this over, the crowd parts in front of me and suddenly I am standing in front of actor Tom Hanks. "It's a pleasure to meet you," I say, reaching out my hand. Hanks asks my name and says he's heard about my book and wants to read it. I tell him I would be honored to send him a copy, and we talk about the movie *Saving Private Ryan,* which I have seen many times.

I finally reconnect with Noel and his family, and together we find Frank Towers and our other friends. We stand at the back of the stage, sharing with one another our favorite moments of the day and talking about the famous personalities we've met. To the right of us we see President Obama's helicopter. Soon the president and first lady approach it, and, after they say a few special goodbyes, Michelle Obama enters the helicopter, followed by the president. Turning toward us, he bids us farewell and disappears from sight. The helicopter door closes and its engines begin to roar. It takes off with two others that serve as decoys, lifting away from the cemetery grounds. We are all waving goodbye. My awe and excitement are not abating. Nothing can ever compare to this day.

I am going to quote what was, for me, the most significant part of President Obama's speech that day:

> We live in a world of competing beliefs and claims about what is true. It is a world of varied religions and cultures and forms of government. In such a world, it is rare for a struggle to emerge that speaks to something universal about humanity. The Second World War did that. No man who shed blood or lost a brother would say war is good. But we all know that this war was essential. For what we faced in the Nazi totalitarianism was not just a battle of competing interests. It was a competing vision of humanity. Nazi ideology sought to subjugate, humiliate, and exterminate. It perpetrated murder on a mass scale, fueled by hatred of those who were deemed different and therefore inferior. It was evil.

My father would understand these words if he had survived to take part in the sixty-fifth anniversary of D-Day. From June 1944 until May 1945 he personally witnessed and suffered under that competing vision of humanity described by President Obama. My father was a simple man who only wanted the opportunity to lead a happy and fulfilling life. From my perspective, he succeeded.

I now fully understand why my father refused to tell me the nitty-gritty details of his war experiences. If he had chosen to do that, especially when I was very young, I believe I might have grown up continuing the cycle of hate. After all, it was my father who those bastard Nazis were abusing. But Dad was very wise and skillful at handling my questions about the war. He'd convince me it was no big deal and that we had plenty of other things to discuss together. Thinking back, I am very impressed that he had the foresight and sensitivity to respond to my questions in this way.

Because of his experiences, my father understood life and its purposes better than most. Several years ago I came upon a quote by Marie

Beyon Ray that perfectly sums up my father and captures the essence of the way my parents raised me: "Begin doing what you want to do now. We are not living in eternity. We have only this moment, sparkling like a star in our hand and melting like a snowflake."

The day my father was liberated from the POW camp he left hating behind and began living. This is the legacy he has left to his children and grandchildren.

ACKNOWLEDGMENTS

This project has been a great adventure for me. During a period of three years, I was privileged to visit many of the areas in England, France, and Germany that experienced the worst of the horror and destruction of World War II. I was equally fortunate to have traveled across America meeting veterans and visiting archives of the era.

I couldn't have completed this book without the help of the amazing people I met along the way. Many of them shared with me their vivid memories of being children in Europe during the war and of hearing their parents' stories about how they tried to escape it. I met entire families who told me about their lives during the war. By listening intently to them, I've been able to better understand my father's war and his struggles. I've reached the certain conclusion that many thousands of stories were as terrible as (or even worse than) his story. I believe that every one of these stories has an important message that needs to be told.

Without question, the person I am most grateful to is my wonderful mother, Eleanore Kurowski Miller. She inspired me to write a book about my father, and the countless hours we spent talking together gave me the framework to do it. Without her willingness to help me, my father's story would have been lost forever. Only days before her death, she said to me: "Write the book." Well, Mom, I did, and it's now finished, thanks to your encouragement and testimony. My mother—God bless her soul—was initially hesitant about dredging up all the hard memories. But over time her interest grew, and she became one of my biggest supporters, eagerly awaiting my weekly visits so that she could tell me more about my father. My mother was very special to me and an invaluable asset to the writing of this book. I told her often in the months before she died that the word "Mom" stands for "Many Outstanding Memories." She loved it.

Writing a book brings new friends and important insights. Thank you first to the seventy extraordinary World War II veterans who spent hours and hours graciously sharing their special stories with me. I also want to extend a special thank-you to Frank Towers, Buster Simmons, Mark Copenhaver, and the other survivors of the 30th Infantry Division who gave me invaluable insights into the Battle for Normandy, Operation Cobra, and the Battle of Mortain. These men also provided me with important information about my father, including details my mother never knew. Gaining this information helped me to better understand the complexities of war and has given me a wider picture of my dad's war experiences.

During the writing of this book, I became very close to my father's brother, a veteran of the Pacific theater. Hank Miller provided me with a continuous stream of memories about my father. I am sad to report his passing, at age eighty-three, in March 2009. I would also like to mention my dad's last remaining sibling, Marlene Bramble, who gave me keen insights into her brother. This was a great help, and it steered me to a lot of information I hadn't known anything about.

I am eternally grateful to my friend Noel Sarrazin, who resides in Mortain, France. Noel was the key to discovering a great many things about my father; he spent countless hours with me exploring all the historic sites of Mortain and the Normandy region. Noel led me across every field, stand of woods, and beach in Normandy to help me visualize the 30th Infantry and my father's trek through the area. Noel also introduced me to many French and American dignitaries who graciously gave me their time. I was deeply honored when Noel agreed to write the foreword for this book. I will always treasure his guidance and friendship. I would also like to thank Noel's wife, Marie-Claire, and their lovely daughter, Anne, for all the great times we had together.

I extend a special thank-you to Bruno Yves, the owner of a photography shop in Mortain. Bruno went through hundreds of original photographs taken by French citizens during World War II, providing me with copies and the rights to use them in my book. Most have never been seen before.

Two people in particular I would like to acknowledge are Michel Desfoux and Walter Frankland III. The mayor of historic Mortain, Desfoux took time out of his day to meet with me on many occasions and generously offered me the resources of his staff. Frankland is the deputy director and chief of staff of the American Battle Monuments Commission—European region. He was instrumental in the success of the Sixty-Fifth Anniversary of D-Day commemoration ceremony and, of course, in my getting the invite from the White House.

I want to acknowledge and thank all the wonderful friends I now have in Mortain. I cherish all my memories of the marvelous French food I ate and the discussions that occurred around their kitchen tables. Because of them, I enjoy French wine and spirits much more than I had previously. I remain amazed at the beauty and quaintness of French country houses.

Turning to the many fine people of Germany, I would like to thank the citizens of Moosburg for all they did to help me understand how Stalag VIIA influenced their town during the war. I had the great pleasure to connect with Werner Schwartz, who lived for many years in Moosburg. Werner was one of the historians who created the Web site Moosburg Online. Although we never met in person, he and I exchanged many e-mails. He answered numerous questions and gave me valuable insights and relevant information on Stalag VIIA. Werner also paved the way for me to meet Bernard Kerscher and Franz Hellmeir, both lifelong citizens of Moosburg, who devoted an entire day to showing me the historic sites of the area. They took me to see where Stalag VIIA once stood and gave me a tour of the Moosburg Museum.

I would also like to acknowledge three of my coworkers at 3M Germany: Mark Pilhofer, Marc Hartwig, and Christophe Arnold. Mark Pilhofer helped to translate many documents from German to English for me. He also cut through red tape to secure archived photos and documents for me to use in my research. The best part of our relationship, though, was our discussions about my book while we sipped Hefe Weizen in the many beer gardens of Germany.

Marc Hartwig took a keen interest in my book and shared with me insights on his family and their struggles during World War II. He gave me much valuable information that helped me to complete the picture of my father's struggles in Germany. The five-hour discussion we had as he drove his BMW very fast on the Autobahn from Munich to Dusseldorf was especially memorable. Whew! We made it!

Christophe Arnold, from France, unselfishly drove many kilometers out of his way to get me from the south of France to Mortain in the week before the D-Day commemoration. Like all of my friends in France, Christophe gave me valuable insights and perspectives on the French and their struggles with the Nazi occupation of Europe. One special event is worth mentioning. Christophe wasn't a patron of the McDonald's fast-food chain. But not only did I make him stop at McDonald's, I also made him navigate the drive-through and eat in his car like we Americans do. To my surprise, Christophe ordered a beer. I had no idea that you could buy a beer at McDonald's, especially with take-out. But, of course, that's the way it is in France.

I must acknowledge the global agencies that supplied documents and archived photographs and, most of all, answered every one of my hundreds of questions. I am forever in the debt of the International Red Cross, in the countries of Germany, France, and America; the YMCA; and the National Archives in College Park, Maryland, and every member of its staff who assisted me during my three grueling days conducting research. I put the staff at the National Archives through so many searches that it still makes my head spin. They responded to every request from me with interest and a smile on their faces.

I would like to thank the International Tracing Service (ITS), the Bergen-Belsen Memorial, the Dachau Concentration Camp and Memorial, the Berlin German War Department records, the American Battle Monuments Commission, and the numerous other smaller agencies within Europe that assisted me.

I extend special thanks to Feiga Weiss, from the Holocaust Memorial Center in Farmington Hills, Michigan, for her support and for her research efforts on my behalf. Critical help for my research also came from Matt Rozel, a very gifted teacher and founder of the World War II Living History Project in Upstate New York. Matt has organized many concentration-camp-survivor reunions. His insights helped me to better understand what my father endured during the time he spent in two prison camps.

I am eternally grateful that I connected with my father's close friend John Chieko. John had also been a POW, in another camp. My father loved John and confided in him, and they shared a special bond. John confirmed what my mother had already told me, and he brought many new stories and events to life that further aided in my writing of this book.

I would like to give a special thanks to the United States Veterans Administration, especially to POW coordinator Wayne Byrum. Wayne clearly understood my cause and paved the way for me to gain access to my father's complete health and war records. This in itself was a major feat.

During the writing of this book, I visited Europe nearly sixteen times, speaking with more than 350 people whose lives have been affected in some way by World War II. So many of these individuals have touched and changed my life forever. I am a blessed man.

Behind every book are the many people who help to make it happen. I am very grateful to Penny Schreiber, my super editor. She is gifted, firm, and concise. When I first asked Penny to read the manuscript, she stopped after fifty pages, concluding that I'd written a term paper. She chose to read on, though, and discovered a compelling tale. Penny agreed to take me on as her client and the rest is history. I am so fortunate to have her behind my story. It is because of her that my book is as good as it is.

I would like to acknowledge Nancy Rabitoy for her many hours of design work on the cover and the interior of the book. The final result has fully captured everything I could have hoped for.

I extend grateful thanks to my good friend from college Chick Hershberger, who has supported me with research, Web site design, and help with publisher requirements. Chick and I have known each other for thirty years and counting. Without his expert help, I would still be staring at a blank Web site.

From the bottom of my heart, I thank my youngest son, Patrick, for the many long hours of support and help he gave me while I was writing this book. Patrick never met my father, who died before he was born. But he now knows his grandfather well as a very special person. What a wonderful legacy for Patrick.

Of course, my most important thank-you goes to my beautiful wife, Colleen. She has stood by me and encouraged me in every way during the arduous ups and downs of researching and writing a book. Behind every good man is a great woman, and Colleen is certainly that. She constantly reminds me of the words she had inscribed on my wedding ring almost thirty years ago: "I won't be bored."

My most profound thank-you goes to my late father, Herbert H. Miller. I am so honored to have been his son. Dad is an example of how the greatest achievements sometimes happen when we least expect them. I am forever grateful for his heroic efforts on behalf of humanity. May he rest in peace and may we meet again under much better circumstances than those the world offers us today.

Robert H. Miller
Canton, Michigan
May 2011

A young Robert Miller peering out between the white pickets of the fence his father built around their yard in the 1950s in Dearborn, Michigan.

ROBERT H. MILLER spent three years researching and writing the story of his father's harrowing nine months as a POW in Germany during World War II. *Hidden Hell: Discovering My Father's POW Diary* is the result of his efforts.

In August 2010, Miller accepted the newly created position of Executive Director of the Patton Foundation. In this role, Miller will oversee the foundation's efforts in America to put into practice General George Patton's concerns for the welfare of American soldiers and their families. Miller will also be working to ensure the continued preservation of the World War II Patton archives, which are located in historic areas of France.

For the last sixteen years Miller has worked in advanced LED lighting and technology design centered on the global auto market. He travels internationally for his work, and he took advantage of time spent in Europe to research and write *Hidden Hell*.

Miller, a professional photographer for thirty-six years, has won several international awards. He lives in Canton, Michigan, with his wife, Colleen. They have five children.